Baseball's Greatest Careers (Non-Pitchers) Compared in 56 Statistical Categories

Second Edition

by

Dale A. Newlin, Jr.

DORRANCE PUBLISHING CO., INC.
PITTSBURGH, PENNSYLVANIA 15222

ISBN # 0-8059-3836-2
Printed in the United States of America

First Printing

For information or to order additional books, please write:
Dorrance Publishing Co., Inc.
643 Smithfield Street
Pittsburgh, Pennsylvania 15222
U.S.A.

Dedication

To Col. and Mrs. Dale A. Newlin, Sr.

Acknowledgments

Thank you to just some of the many fans who have furnished enthusiasm and interest for this four year project: Don Huse, Dorothy Newlin, Don Elliot, Bruce Winston, Dick Zitzman, the "1-2-3 Club", Ralph Horton, Bob Broeg, S.F.M., Bob Burnes, Joe Phillips, Rick Hines, Mark Alvarez, Wilma Chase, and to anyone else who has ever, or will ever, compare baseball players. Comments and suggestions are welcome.

Contents

Speed

Other

Appendix

Foreword

"He was the best I've ever seen!"

"He could beat you with his arm, on the base paths, or at the bat!"

"The greatest hitter who ever lived!"

"The most exciting player ever!"

"He was the greatest all-around player!"

Opinion will always be a key part of our national pastime and go a long way to help us pass the winter waiting for the new season. Baseball is unique in that it inspires (subjective) appraisals, such as those listed above, and also produces more (objective) statistical evidence than any other sport. This book was compiled as a backdrop to the inevitable discussions as to who was "better"—Mantle or Mays, Musial or Williams, Cobb or Wagner. I have attempted to provide as many facts about as many facets of the game as there are available. I measure career numbers, peak performance (three best seasons), speed, defense, (by position), most valuable player (MVP) votes, how often one led the league in any statistic (stat), and adjustments for the different eras.

About the Categories

Categories 1 through 11 are widely accepted career offensive statistics. Of the players in the career runs scored category, Ty Cobb scored the most and is given 100 points. Lou Gehrig scored 1,888 runs, which is 84 percent of Cobb's total percentage, and is therefore given eighty-four points. Players are scored as a percentage of the leader's score in each category. Any two players can now easily be compared. However, an objection is that Hank Aaron hit 755 home runs, 41 more than Babe Ruth, but Ruth batted 4,000 fewer times than Aaron. Categories 1 through 11 measure longevity, consistency, and durability. But what about DiMaggio and Williams missing time due to the war?

Categories 12 through 23 set measures per at bat. Now all the players are on a level field. In home runs Babe Ruth is number one and Ted Williams is number two.

Categories 24 through 29 measure defense. The players are measured against the best at their respective position by a Hall of Famer. The best fielding average by a Hall of Fame centerfielder is .985 by Duke Snider. The four centerfielders in this category are then compared to his score. To emphasize this, I also include errors as a percentage of total chances. (This is a reciprocal number to fielding average but makes the scores more noticeable). For the first basemen I have added assists as a percentage of total chances to check their throwing ability to other bases.

Categories 30 through 35 are measures of speed referred to by Bill James in his book, *Historical Baseball Abstract*: stolen base attempts as a percentage of times on base; stolen base percentage; non-home runs scored as a percentage of times on base; ground into double plays; triples and range. All collectively give an indication of speed.

Categories 36 through 37 are a collection of famous measurements of a ball players ability. Special mention is made of Category 37: Total Average. Some fans have sought a way to adjust performance from era to era. In other words a .300 average in 1968, a pitcher's year, might be more valuable than a .300 average in 1930 when the whole league hit .300. Leo Leahy addresses this in his book *Lumber Men*, and comes up with an Offensive Quotient (OQ). This measures total bases divided by outs divided by the league that year. Next to the Total Average stat by Mr. Boswell I have included how the same players were ranked by Mr. Leahy's OQ. You can see the similarities. For those who insist on adjusting for the era, Categories 44 and 48 measure peak performance—a player's three best years—instead of career performance.

Categories 49 through 52 are my way of measuring a player versus his peers. Using ten offensive categories, every time a player led the league he scored 5 points; finishing second scored 4 points, etc. with fifth place scoring 1 point. There is a career total and a per year average total. Defensively I only scored the first and second finishers in a category. Finishing first in assists among centerfielders scored 5 points, second scored four points, and third scored 0.

How often was a player among the leaders in his league in batting and fielding his position? Category 54 is a favorite because it takes into account people who actually saw them play, day in and day out.

One note about defense. In Bill James's comparison of Mays and Mantle, the consensus was that Mays was the better fielder and Mantle the better hitter. Now the question is, how much difference does one fielder make over the course of the season? The difference between the best defensive team (the least runs allowed per season) and the worst (most runs allowed) throughout baseball history is about 250 runs per year. Factor in all the variables, great throwing catcher, great double play combination, relief pitching, starting pitching, etc. And we find that the difference between a very, very, very good outfielder and a very good outfielder might be as little as 5 or 6 runs.

As a different stat would be presented, a new source would be brought into the equation. We used the *Baseball Encyclopedia*, a new publication by Pete Palmer called *Total Baseball*, Bill James's *Historical Baseball Abstract*, (the best baseball book I have ever read), *Earl Weaver's Baseball Hall of Fame League*, *Lumber Men* by Leo Leahy, *Baseball's Best Pitchers* by Ralph Horton, and any other publications, records, or viewpoints we could find.

This book contains nearly every published statistic available. Of fifty-six total categories, each were weighted equally: thirty-three are about batting, ten are about fielding, seven are about speed and range, six are considered all around measurements.

How was it weighted by percentage?

Batting 59%

Fielding............. 18%

Speed and Range 12%

All Around 11%

The reader must supply any subjective opinions and aesthetic values. Some consideration besides style points might be given to work ethic, influence in the dugout, influence in the clubhouse, and Was he a team player? Finally, some might observe that statistics do not tell the whole story. True. Also, the reader may disagree with the premise of any one individual category, as I do myself with one or two. But with over a twenty year career in studying the game of baseball and players as great as these, this cumulative, statistical account certainly points in the right direction.

My conclusion is that Stan Musial's baseball career (all around hitting and fielding at three positions)* is the best since Babe Ruth. It comes as no surprise that Ted Williams was a great hitter. Willie Mays had the most exciting combination of defense and power. Honus Wagner would be a wise first pick when drafting an all-time rotisserie team. In total, Williams and Gehrig are just too close to call. Tris Speaker was the greatest outfielder. Take your pick at second base among Hornsby, Lajoie, and Collins, here you might need some of the subjective criteria we talked about earlier. Eddie Collins's ranking surprised some younger fans. Babe Ruth, true to old-timers' accounts was a good outfielder. An appendix with interesting background is included.

*Stan Musial won three MVPs, each while playing a different position: 1943, right field; 1946, first base; 1948 left field.

Categories 1 through 11 are composed of traditional career numbers that measure endurance, durability, the most prolific player, the greatest hitter of home runs, doubles, etc. As Bob Broeg explains in his book, *Super Stars of Baseball*, when speaking about the difference between Hank Aaron and Babe Ruth, Aaron is really the greatest hitter of home runs. He was the most prolific, whereas Ruth would be the greatest home run hitter, because Aaron batted 4,000 or more times than Ruth. Note that besides Ty Cobb and Babe Ruth, of the next four in ranking of career runs scored, Hank Aaron had thirteen consecutive years in which he scored more than 100 runs. Willie Mays had twelve consecutive years in which he scored over 100 runs, Musial had eleven consecutive years, and Lou Gehrig had thirteen consecutive years in which he scored over 100 runs. So besides producing career stats, they were also incredibly consistent year after year. Besides scoring 131 runs in his rookie year, Ted Williams never scored fewer than 124 runs his first eight years through 1949, and that includes taking three years off in the service and coming right back scoring 125 runs. So his first eight years are all over 100 runs. In 1950 he played in only 89 games and scored 82 runs. In 1951 he had another 109-run season. At the age of thirty-nine, in 1957, besides winning a batting title, he also scored another 96 runs.

Category 1
Career Runs Scored

	Score	%
Cobb	2,245	100.00
Ruth	2,174	96.80
Aaron	2,174	96.80
Mays	2,062	91.80
Musial	1,949	86.80
Gehrig	1,888	84.00
Speaker	1,882	83.80
Ott	1,859	82.80
F. Robinson	1,829	81.40
Collins	1,819	81.00
Williams	1,798	80.00
Gehringer	1,774	79.00
Foxx	1,751	77.90
Wagner	1,736	77.30
Mantle	1,677	74.60
Morgan	1,650	73.49
Hornsby	1,579	70.30
Schmidt	1,506	67.00
Lajoie	1,504	66.90
DiMaggio	1,390	61.90

With Category 2 we hit our first snag. The first four on the list of fewest strike-outs—Speaker, Collins, Wagner, and Cobb—conceivably had the fewest official strikeouts because, for several years during their careers, strikeouts were not counted as a statistic. So the scores they have are admittedly incomplete. I have estimated that based on the years of complete statistics Speaker would have finished with around 276 career strikeouts, Collins 375 and Cobb 499. Wagner was more difficult and would have finished further down the list than he does here, but Speaker and Collins would have finished in the same places they do now. I am uncomfortable with using estimated numbers for this, and yet, I want to give credit to batters who struck out very rarely, so I'm going ahead and using only the true recorded strikeouts that are listed in the record books. Speaker and Collins still would have been number one and number two, so Speaker would be the category leader with 100 points. Ball players who struck out rarely, and who we will see later on hit for home runs, are DiMaggio, Musial, Williams, Gehrig, and Ott—all under 1,000 strikeouts in their careers.

Category 2
Fewest Career Strikeouts

	Score	%
Speaker	220	100.00
Collins	286	76.90
Wagner	327	67.20
Cobb	357	61.60
DiMaggio	369	59.60
Gehringer	372	59.13
Hornsby	679	32.40
Musial	696	31.60
Williams	709	31.00
Gehrig	789	27.80
Ott	896	24.55
Morgan	1,015	21.67
Foxx	1,311	16.70
Ruth	1,330	16.50
Aaron	1,383	15.90
Mays	1,526	14.40
F. Robinson	1,532	14.30
Mantle	1,710	12.80
Schmidt	1,883	11.68
Lajoie	—	—

In Category 3 we find that some interesting highlights appear. For instance, Tris Speaker, the leader in this category, never had a year in the twenty full seasons he played where he hit under twenty doubles in a year. He had five years of over fifty doubles and once in 1923, he had 59 doubles. Ty Cobb, in the full seasons he played, never had a year without double digits. However, he had some years that dropped below 20. Stan Musial, second in the category, never had a year in his career where he finished under double digits and he had three seasons where he hit 50 doubles. His high mark was in 1953 when he hit 53 doubles. Lajoie, from even the first year when he played 39 games, never hit less than a double digit number. In this category we first begin to notice, even though he played only thirteen years and had far fewer career at bats, DiMaggio does not automatically finish last in each of these categories.

Category 3
Career Doubles

	Score	%
Speaker	792	100.00
Musial	725	91.50
Cobb	724	91.40
Lajoie	657	82.90
Wagner	640	80.80
Aaron	624	78.70
Gehringer	574	72.47
Hornsby	541	68.30
Gehrig	534	67.40
F. Robinson	528	66.60
Williams	525	66.20
Mays	523	66.00
Ruth	506	63.80
Ott	488	61.60
Foxx	458	57.80
Morgan	449	56.69
Collins	437	55.10
Schmidt	408	51.50
DiMaggio	389	49.10
Mantle	344	43.40

As far as triples are concerned, Ty Cobb, who leads the category, had thirteen consecutive years of hitting triples numbering in the double-digits. We notice, too, that in the Career Doubles and Career Triples categories, the names that appear at the top of both lists—Cobb, Wagner, Speaker, and Musial—really have reputations for leaving the batters box on the run and having some speed in the early part of their careers. In the Career Triples category, Musial also owns the often quoted statistic of being the only ball player to have more than 170 triples and 170 career home runs, showing a blend of both speed and power. He may be closer to our modern day players in terms of time, but statistically speaking he is a throwback to the days of players like Cobb, Wagner, and Speaker. Again in career triples, even with fewer at bats and opportunities, DiMaggio was far from automatically finishing last. He is high up on the list of triples.

Category 4
Career Triples

	Score	%
Cobb	295	100.00
Wagner	252	85.40
Speaker	222	75.20
Collins	186	63.00
Musial	177	60.00
Hornsby	169	57.20
Gehrig	163	55.20
Lajoie	163	55.20
Gehringer	146	49.49
Mays	140	47.40
Ruth	136	46.10
DiMaggio	131	44.40
Foxx	125	42.30
Aaron	98	33.20
Morgan	96	32.54
Ott	72	24.40
Mantle	72	24.40
F. Robinson	72	24.40
Williams	71	24.00
Schmidt	59	20.00

Here are the greatest hitters of home runs. We notice Aaron with 755 home runs, but he batted 4,000 more times than Babe Ruth. Ted Williams hit 521 home runs and DiMaggio hit 361, but both missed three years due to time in the service. Again, that will be addressed in another category. Note the power of Joe Morgan; later on in our report we will see him finishing high in other power categories also. Then of course there are the dead-ball era players finishing toward the bottom of the list. Speaking of longevity and consistency, Hank Aaron had eight years in which he hit over 40 home runs. Babe Ruth had eleven years in which he hit over 40 home runs and four years in which he hit over 50. Willie Mays had six years in which he hit more than 40 home runs; Lou Gehrig had five years in which he hit more than 40; Jimmie Foxx had five years; and Stan Musial, with 475 home runs, had the most home runs of anyone who never led the league in home runs in any one year.

Category 5
Career Home Runs

	Score	%
Aaron	755	100.00
Ruth	714	94.50
Mays	660	87.40
F. Robinson	586	77.60
Schmidt	548	72.50
Mantle	536	70.90
Foxx	534	70.70
Williams	521	69.00
Ott	511	67.60
Gehrig	493	65.20
Musial	475	62.90
DiMaggio	361	47.80
Hornsby	301	39.80
Morgan	268	35.49
Gehringer	184	24.37
Speaker	117	15.40
Cobb	117	15.40
Wagner	101	13.30
Lajoie	83	10.90
Collins	47	6.20

Lou Gehrig and Jimmie Foxx each had thirteen consecutive years in which they batted in over 100 RBIs. Ted Williams, just like in his runs scored, had a great rookie year, 1939, with 145 RBIs. Again in 1957, at the age of thirty-nine, Williams batted in 87 RBIs. Joe DiMaggio, who served three years in the service and had 1,200 fewer at bats than Mickey Mantle, drove in more runs than Mantle.

Category 6
Career Runs Batted In (RBIs)

	Score	%
Aaron	2,297	100.00
Ruth	2,209	96.10
Gehrig	1,990	86.60
Musial	1,951	84.90
Cobb	1,937	84.30
Foxx	1,922	83.60
Mays	1,903	82.80
Ott	1,860	80.90
Williams	1,839	80.00
F. Robinson	1,812	78.80
Wagner	1,732	75.40
Lajoie	1,599	69.60
Schmidt	1,595	69.40
Hornsby	1,584	68.90
DiMaggio	1,537	66.90
Speaker	1,529	66.50
Mantle	1,509	65.60
Gehringer	1,427	62.12
Collins	1,299	56.50
Morgan	1,133	49.32

Willie Mays and Lou Gehrig each had thirteen consecutive years of over 300 total bases. For those concerned about comparing eras—for example the live ball in the 1920s and 1930s versus the other eras—there are only ten players who have amassed over 400 total bases in a single season. The only players who didn't do it during the 1920s or 1930s were Jim Rice and Stan Musial, who in 1948 had 429 total bases. Hank Aaron, the leader in this category, had fifteen years where he had more than 300 total bases in a single season!

Category 7
Career Total Bases

	Score	%
Aaron	6,856	100.00
Musial	6,134	89.40
Mays	6,066	88.40
Cobb	5,855	85.30
Ruth	5,793	84.40
F. Robinson	5,373	78.30
Speaker	5,101	74.40
Gehrig	5,060	73.80
Ott	5,041	73.50
Foxx	4,956	72.20
Williams	4,884	71.20
Wagner	4,862	70.90
Hornsby	4,712	68.70
Mantle	4,511	65.70
Lajoie	4,474	65.20
Schmidt	4,404	64.20
Collins	4,260	62.10
Gehringer	4,257	62.09
Morgan	3,962	57.78
DiMaggio	3,948	57.50

We find the doubles and triples hitters, Musial, Cobb, and Speaker sandwiched in between the big home run hitters. This calls attention to the fact that on many of these career statistics so far we find Babe Ruth very high in the standing with thousands of at bats less than the leader of the category. In Category 8, Aaron has 4,000 more at bats than Babe Ruth, yet Ruth is third in career extra base hits.

Category 8
Career Extra Base Hits

	Score	%
Aaron	1,477	100.00
Musial	1,377	93.20
Ruth	1,356	91.80
Mays	1,323	89.50
Gehrig	1,190	80.50
F. Robinson	1,186	80.20
Cobb	1,136	76.90
Speaker	1,131	76.50
Foxx	1,117	75.60
Williams	1,117	75.60
Ott	1,071	72.50
Schmidt	1,015	68.70
Hornsby	1,011	68.40
Wagner	993	67.20
Mantle	952	64.40
Gehringer	904	61.20
Lajoie	903	61.10
DiMaggio	881	59.60
Morgan	813	55.04
Collins	670	45.30

This is just one of the many hitting categories in which we see Ruth and Williams at the top. Here we see evidence of the many stories about the perfectionist, Ted Williams, waiting for or being discriminating in the pitches at which he swung. Also, for the first time, but not the last in the report, we see Joe Morgan appearing very high in the standings.

Category 9
Career Bases on Balls

	Score	%
Ruth	2,056	100.00
Williams	2,019	98.20
Morgan	1,865	90.71
Mantle	1,733	84.20
Ott	1,708	83.00
Musial	1,599	77.70
Gehrig	1,508	73.30
Schmidt	1,507	73.20
Collins	1,499	72.90
Mays	1,464	71.20
Foxx	1,452	70.60
F. Robinson	1,420	69.00
Aaron	1,402	68.10
Speaker	1,381	67.10
Cobb	1,249	60.70
Gehringer	1,186	57.68
Hornsby	1,038	50.40
Wagner	963	46.80
DiMaggio	790	38.40
Lajoie	516	25.00

Although later in this book we will be talking about the variance in style of play between the different eras in baseball, here is one instance where we need to be careful in considering these different eras.

As many do today, considering stolen bases as a measure of speed can be deceiving. Comparing whether or not the stolen base was utilized by teams in any particular era helps to provide a more objective measure. Obviously in the early eras there were quite a few more stolen bases. In 1948 for example, Musial stole 7 bases, while the whole St. Louis Cardinal team—known as a fast, smart, defensive team—stole all of 24 bases. But we will address speed using a combination of categories later on.

For now, here are the career leaders in stolen bases; and again we see Joe Morgan right up there with early era base stealers like Cobb, Collins, Wagner, and Speaker. Many people will comment on the all around ability of Willie Mays and we see proof of that here with his 660 home runs and 338 stolen bases—the best combination of speed and power that we have seen in this book. The 1940s teams just didn't use the stolen base with their big marquee players, Musial, DiMaggio, and Williams.

Category 10
Career Stolen Bases

	Score	%
Cobb	891	100.00
Collins	744	83.50
Wagner	722	81.00
Morgan	689	77.32
Speaker	434	48.70
Lajoie	380	42.60
Mays	338	37.90
Aaron	240	26.90
F. Robinson	204	22.80
Gehringer	181	20.31
Schmidt	174	19.50
Mantle	153	17.10
Hornsby	135	15.10
Ruth	123	13.80
Gehrig	102	11.40
Ott	89	9.90
Foxx	87	9.70
Musial	78	8.70
DiMaggio	30	3.30
Williams	24	2.60

Here are some more examples of endurance, longevity, and consistency. Ty Cobb had nine years where he had over 200 hits a season. Stan Musial had six years with over 200 hits and four years with over 190 hits. Charlie Gehringer had seven years with 200 hits and Lou Gehrig had eight years with 200 hits or more, and one year with 198. Rogers Hornsby had seven years with at least 200 hits. Mickey Mantle never had a 200 hit season, nor did Ted Williams.

For those who wonder about the differences of the home ball park versus the road ball park (if there ever was an advantage to the home park), those numbers are available. Babe Ruth, for instance, during his career actually played one fewer game on the road than at home and had 1,475 hits on the road and 1,398 hits at home. Mickey Mantle finished his career with 1,210 hits at home and 1,205 hits on the road, and Stan Musial, over the length of his career, had 1,815 hits at home and 1,815 hits on the road.

Category 11
Career Hits

	Score	%
Cobb	4,190	100.00
Aaron	3,771	90.00
Musial	3,630	86.60
Speaker	3,514	83.80
Wagner	3,415	81.50
Collins	3,310	78.90
Mays	3,283	78.30
Lajoie	3,242	77.30
F. Robinson	2,943	70.20
Hornsby	2,930	69.90
Ott	2,876	68.60
Ruth	2,873	68.50
Gehringer	2,839	67.75
Gehrig	2,721	64.90
Williams	2,654	63.30
Foxx	2,646	63.10
Morgan	2,517	60.07
Mantle	2,415	57.60
Schmidt	2,234	53.30
DiMaggio	2,214	52.80

Categories 12 through 23 measure per at bat in these respects: the most prodigious, the greatest doubles hitter, the greatest home run hitter, etc. These categories illustrate peak performance and adjust for missing at bats because of the service and injuries. The playing field is now level for those with shortened careers. Already we see a difference in the rankings compared to Category 1. Now we see Ruth moving up to first place, Gehrig is second, Williams is third, and Foxx moves up with Mantle and DiMaggio. We see how efficient they were when measured per at bat.

Category 12
Most Runs Per at Bat

	Score	%
Ruth.	.258	100.00
Gehrig.	.235	91.00
Williams	.233	90.30
Foxx	.215	83.40
Mantle.	.206	79.80
DiMaggio	.203	78.90
Gehringer	.200	77.60
Cobb	.196	75.90
Ott.	.196	75.90
Hornsby	.193	74.80
Mays	.189	73.20
Speaker.	.184	71.50
Collins.	.182	70.80
F. Robinson.	.182	70.80
Schmidt.	.180	69.80
Morgan	.177	68.93
Musial.	.177	68.60
Aaron	.175	67.80
Wagner	.166	64.30
Lajoie	.156	60.70

Because strikeouts were not being calculated consistently during some of the early players' careers, I've stayed with the actual number of strikeouts. For instance, if we estimate Speaker's strikeouts that he would have had during the years in which they weren't counted, his score of 46 at bats without a strikeout would actually have been 35; Collins's would be about 29; Cobb and Wagner would also have lower numbers. But Speaker, Collins, and Cobb would still be in the same relative ranking. They would still be first, second, and third, though the numbers would be estimates. Musial with 15.76 at bats before striking out, still has the best score of anyone who hit 400 home runs or more during his career.

Category 13
Number at Bats Before Striking Out

	Score	%
Speaker	46.34	100.00
Collins	34.78	75.06
Cobb	32.02	69.09
Wagner	31.89	68.80
Gehringer	23.81	51.39
DiMaggio	18.48	39.89
Musial	15.76	34.00
Hornsby	12.03	25.96
Ott	10.55	22.76
Gehrig	10.14	21.88
Williams	9.20	19.85
Morgan	9.13	19.72
Aaron	8.93	19.27
Mays	7.13	15.38
F. Robinson	6.53	14.09
Ruth	6.31	13.61
Foxx	6.20	13.37
Mantle	4.73	10.20
Schmidt	4.43	9.57
Lajoie	—	—

We again see Williams and Gehrig moving up higher. For those DiMaggio fans who were certain about his ability, these categories measuring per at bat vindicate your judgements. You see him move much higher in each of these. We can only speculate as to what a career of twenty years, rather than thirteen would have done to his gross career totals. Here, looking at his production per at bat, you can see why he was regarded so highly by his peers.

Category 14
Most Doubles Per at Bat

	Score	%
Speaker	.0770	100.00
Lajoie	.0680	88.90
Williams	.0680	88.30
Gehrig	.0667	86.60
Musial	.0660	85.70
Hornsby	.0660	85.70
Gehringer	.0640	84.13
Cobb	.0633	82.20
Wagner	.0610	79.20
Ruth	.0600	77.90
DiMaggio	.0570	74.00
Foxx	.0560	73.10
F. Robinson	.0520	68.50
Ott	.0510	66.20
Aaron	.0500	64.90
Schmidt	.0480	63.40
Morgan	.0480	62.85
Mays	.0480	62.30
Collins	.0430	57.00
Mantle	.0420	54.50

We see what might be a surprise to some—Rogers Hornsby and Lou Gehrig hitting lots of triples, but there they are. Once again DiMaggio finishes higher. Also in Category 15, we find that the last first baseman to lead his league in triples was Stan Musial in 1946.

Category 15
Most Triples Per at Bat

	Score	%
Cobb	.02500	100.00
Wagner	.02400	96.00
Speaker	.02170	86.80
Hornsby	.02000	82.70
Gehrig	.02000	80.00
DiMaggio	.01920	76.82
Collins	.01860	74.70
Lajoie	.01600	67.90
Gehringer	.01600	65.91
Ruth	.01619	64.70
Musial	.01613	64.50
Foxx	.01500	61.40
Mays	.01200	48.00
Morgan	.01000	41.39
Williams	.00900	36.00
Mantle	.00800	32.00
F. Robinson	.00717	28.70
Schmidt	.00705	28.20
Ott	.00700	28.00
Aaron	.00700	28.00

When we rank home runs per at bat, we might ask: What if they all played the same number of games and there were no absences from military service and injury? Playing the same number of games, how would they rank as home run hitters? I think that in the case of the first ten or so players we have a list of what might be the *All-Time Home Run Derby* winners. That would be a fairly accurate ranking. From DiMaggio on down we see all contact hitters.

Category 16
Most Home Runs Per at Bat

	Score	%
Ruth	.085	100.00
Williams	.067	78.80
Mantle	.066	77.60
Foxx	.065	76.40
Schmidt	.065	76.40
Gehrig	.061	71.70
Aaron	.061	71.70
Mays	.060	70.50
F. Robinson	.058	68.20
Ott	.054	63.50
DiMaggio	.052	61.10
Musial	.043	50.50
Hornsby	.036	42.30
Morgan	.028	33.98
Gehringer	.020	24.43
Speaker	.011	12.90
Cobb	.010	11.70
Wagner	.009	10.50
Lajoie	.008	9.40
Collins	.004	4.70

From here to the end of the per at bat categories we see Ruth and Williams at the top of almost every category; DiMaggio finishes much higher; and Gehrig, Foxx, and Hornsby do well also.

Category 17
Most RBIs Per at Bat

	Score	%
Ruth	.263	100.00
Gehrig	.248	94.20
Williams	.238	90.40
Foxx	.236	89.80
DiMaggio	.225	85.60
Ott	.196	74.50
Hornsby	.193	73.60
Schmidt	.190	72.60
Mantle	.186	70.70
Aaron	.185	70.30
F. Robinson	.181	68.80
Musial	.177	67.30
Mays	.174	66.10
Cobb	.169	64.20
Lajoie	.166	63.40
Wagner	.166	63.10
Gehringer	.161	61.23
Speaker	.149	56.60
Collins	.130	49.60
Morgan	.122	46.43

After his first season in 1905, when he only played 41 games to the end of his career, Ty Cobb never batted under .300. Stan Musial had sixteen consecutive .300 seasons. (He holds the National League record.) Ted Williams had only one year where he hit under .300 and, to reiterate, at the age of thirty-nine, in 1957, he hit .388. Willie Mays failed to hit .300 in any of his last eight seasons. For his career Stan Musial batted .331 versus left handed pitching and .331 versus right handed pitching, and was the last player to hit .400 on the road in 1948.

Category 18
Career Batting Average

	Score	%
Cobb	.366	100.00
Hornsby	.358	97.80
Speaker	.345	94.20
Williams	.344	93.90
Ruth	.340	93.40
Gehrig	.340	93.40
Lajoie	.338	92.30
Collins	.333	90.90
Musial	.331	90.40
Wagner	.327	89.30
Foxx	.325	88.70
DiMaggio	.325	88.70
Gehringer	.320	87.19
Aaron	.305	83.30
Ott	.304	83.00
Mays	.302	82.50
Mantle	.298	81.40
F. Robinson	.294	80.30
Morgan	.271	73.84
Schmidt	.267	72.90

Slugging Average is defined as the total bases divided by at bats. Here is the familiar sight of Ruth and Williams at the top of the list. DiMaggio and Musial rank high without being home run hitters and the throw back players, the early era players, are on the lower part of the list. Twelve times during his career Ted Williams had a slugging average of over .600. Even his last year in 1960, at forty plus years of age, his slugging average was .645. For three years he had a slugging average of over .700. Babe Ruth had thirteen years where his slugging average was over .600, seven of those years over .700, and two exceeded .800. Stan Musial holds the highest single season slugging average in the National League since 1941 at .702, which is also the highest National League slugging average for a left-hander ever. Gehrig and Foxx each have nine years in which their slugging average was over .600.

Category 19
Career Slugging Average

	Score	%
Ruth.	.690	100.00
Williams	.634	91.80
Gehrig	.632	91.50
Foxx	.609	88.20
DiMaggio	.579	83.90
Hornsby	.577	83.60
Musial	.559	81.00
Mays	.557	80.70
Mantle	.557	80.70
Aaron	.555	80.40
F. Robinson.	.537	77.80
Ott	.533	77.24
Schmidt	.527	76.30
Cobb	.512	74.20
Speaker	.500	72.40
Gehringer	.480	69.56
Wagner	.468	67.80
Lajoie	.467	67.60
Collins.	.428	62.00
Morgan	.427	61.88

This is the percentage of times a player gets on base. Once again, we see Williams, Ruth, and Gehrig at the top of our list. What an interesting ranking in this category! We find a great home run hitter, Ruth, second on the list, and another great home run hitter, Hank Aaron, last on the list, and power hitters and contact hitters mixed all the way through. We see Schmidt and Mays mixed with Wagner and Joe Morgan; Musial next to Mantle; and Speaker and Cobb next to Jimmie Foxx. Of course Ted Williams and Babe Ruth received many bases on balls during their careers while Williams's legendary batting eye sought almost perfect pitches. As far as an on base percentage for Ted Williams, he led the league twelve times and six times his on base percentage was .500 or higher. Babe Ruth also had five years when his on base percentage was over .500. Ted Williams had seven consecutive years when his on base percentage was over .400 and Lou Gehrig had thirteen consecutive years with an on base percentage over .400. Conversely, Hank Aaron had only three years where his on base percentage exceeded .400.

Category 20
Career on Base Percentage

	Score	%
Williams	.483	100.00
Ruth	.474	98.10
Gehrig	.447	92.50
Hornsby	.434	89.80
Cobb	.432	89.40
Speaker	.428	88.60
Foxx	.428	88.60
Collins	.424	87.70
Mantle	.423	87.50
Musial	.418	86.50
Ott	.414	85.71
Gehringer	.404	83.64
DiMaggio	.398	82.40
Morgan	.395	81.78
F. Robinson	.392	81.10
Mays	.387	80.10
Schmidt	.384	79.50
Wagner	.380	78.60
Lajoie	.378	78.20
Aaron	.373	77.20

Once again Ruth, Gehrig, and Williams are number one. DiMaggio, on a per at bat basis moves up to number six. Musial and Hornsby are ahead of the power hitters and the contact hitters are at the end.

Category 21
Most Extra Base Hits Per at Bat

	Score	%
Ruth.	.161	100.00
Gehrig	.148	91.90
Williams	.144	89.40
Foxx	.137	85.20
Ott	.133	82.60
DiMaggio	.129	80.20
Musial	.125	77.60
Hornsby	.123	76.80
Schmidt.	.121	75.48
Mays	.121	75.10
F. Robinson.	.118	73.60
Mantle.	.117	72.60
Speaker	.110	68.90
Aaron	.110	68.30
Gehringer	.102	63.35
Cobb	.099	61.40
Wagner	.095	59.00
Lajoie	.094	58.40
Morgan	.087	54.43
Collins.	.067	41.60

Here's another high finish by Joe Morgan who had nine consecutive years of 40 stolen bases or more. Wagner had eight consecutive years of 40 stolen bases or more and eighteen years (consecutive) of 20 stolen bases or more. Eddie Collins had six consecutive years of 40 stolen bases or more.

Category 22
Most Stolen Bases Per at Bat

	Score	%
Cobb	.077	100.00
Collins	.074	97.10
Morgan	.074	96.45
Wagner	.069	89.60
Speaker	.042	55.20
Lajoie	.039	51.40
Mays	.031	40.20
Schmidt	.020	27.00
Gehringer	.020	26.53
F. Robinson	.020	26.40
Aaron	.019	24.60
Mantle	.018	23.30
Hornsby	.016	21.40
Ruth	.014	18.10
Gehrig	.012	15.50
Foxx	.010	13.80
Ott	.009	11.68
Musial	.007	9.00
DiMaggio	.004	5.70
Williams	.003	3.80

In his career Ted Williams had eleven years in which he received more than 100 walks, one year with 96, and one year with 98. Mickey Mantle had ten years with more than 100 walks, one year with 99, including 107 and 106 walks the last two years that he played. Babe Ruth had thirteen years with over 100 walks. Lou Gehrig had eleven years with over 100 and only one full season did he play in which he received less than 90 walks. Joe Morgan, who finished very high in these categories, had eight years with over 100 walks and three years with over 90.

In summary, looking back over our first twenty-three traditional offensive categories, we find that once we calculate statistics on a per at bat basis any disadvantage that Joe DiMaggio had for playing fewer games, fewer at bats, etc., disappears—he finishes in the top half or better of these categories. Williams and Ruth, on a per at bat basis, are continually among the top two or three hitters. In the career categories (the first eleven), Musial and Aaron finish high in career numbers. When we get to the per at bat numbers, Musial still stays in the top half, or better, of the categories (except for the stolen bases); Aaron, however, drops down to the bottom half of the categories.

Category 23
Most Bases on Balls Per at Bat

	Score	%
Williams	.262	100.00
Ruth	.244	93.10
Mantle	.213	81.20
Morgan	.201	76.73
Gehrig	.188	71.70
Schmidt	.180	68.80
Ott	.180	68.70
Foxx	.178	68.10
Collins	.150	57.50
Musial	.145	55.30
F. Robinson	.141	53.80
Speaker	.135	51.50
Mays	.134	51.10
Gehringer	.133	51.09
Hornsby	.127	48.40
DiMaggio	.115	44.20
Aaron	.113	43.10
Cobb	.109	41.60
Wagner	.092	35.10
Lajoie	.053	20.50

Now let's move on and take a stab at what is generally regarded as the most difficult aspect of baseball in which to accumulate meaningful data—defensive ability. If we look at our first page on defensive stats we are looking at the history of baseball as one long continuation. In other words, we are not comparing eras, astro turf, glove size, or quality of equipment. This stat will be our first try at defensive stats without regard to era. As a means of comparison, because the top performer in any one category gets 100 points and everyone is measured against that, we have six different defensive categories: Category 24, Fielding Average; Category 25, Double Plays per game; Category 26, Assists per game; Category 27, Put Outs per game; Category 28 is for first basemen to measure their throwing arm, Assists as a Percentage of Total Chances and Category 29 is Errors as a Percentage of Total Chances per game.

To begin the comparison we list a break-down of the players in the far left hand column on page 27. Then we take the high score from a Hall of Famer at that position. For instance, fielding average: The best fielding average by a Hall of Famer playing primarily at center field was Duke Snider with .985. This becomes the basis for our comparison. Duke Snider's .985 equals 100 points. We can see down the column what the highest score is at each position on page 26.

As we go through and compare the six categories we note that there is quite a variety of players from different eras. We find that Ed Delahanty is represented in double plays for the left fielders. Showing up for the second basemen we have Frankie Frisch and Jackie Robinson. For shortstops we have Wagner to Louis Aparicio. At third base we have Jimmy Collins and Brooks Robinson. In right field we have Sam Rice and Al Kaline and in center field we have Tris Speaker, Lloyd Waner and Duke Snider. So the different eras are represented throughout the statistics in these categories. For example, in right field Al Kaline had the highest fielding average with .986.

If we look on the table where the outfielders are listed we see at the top three right fielders and Mel Ott at the bottom of the page, also in right field. We see that if Al Kaline receives 100 points for his .986, Hank Aaron's .980 comes next at 98.3, babe Ruth at 98.1- not very much of a difference. That is when we move to Category 29. (Skip ahead to number 29 on the far right hand side of page 27.) We see that if we just measure the errors per total chances, the relationship stays the same. Aaron is ahead of Ruth but behind Frank Robinson (only in the fielding average). Here the discrepancy, the variance, between the percentages becomes much more meaningful. Now we see Aaron at 68.2 points, Ruth at 41.7, and Frank Robinson, who had a higher fielding average than both of them in Category 24, now has 84.8 points. There is a more meaningful relationship between the numbers by using both fielding averages and the errors per total chances. Of course we have defensive stats using the same procedure for the infielders on the next page, and they are all ranked against the top performing Hall of Fame infielder at their respective positions, as well. Now we have a display of the game as if it was basically the same from 1900 to 1990, and we can look at all players without regard to eras.

Once that was done, however, knowledgeable fans such as Joe Phillips, editor of The Glove Collector, mentioned that modern players have higher fielding averages with many fewer chances because by 1970 there were two and a half times as many strikeouts as there were in the earlier days. So the modern players are going to be making fewer errors, taking fewer chances, and therefore having a higher fielding average. For instance, on second base, just a glance at the stats shows that these players were basically even. Yet many observers who saw them play would say that there was no comparison between Eddie Collins and Rogers Hornsby as far as fielding.

So this was our first try at defensive statistics covering the whole history of the game. We will return to defense later as more thought is given, but we include these numbers as traditional baseball statistics measuring the players against the best in each position of the Hall of Fame players. As a note on the outfield, we find that upon delving into the defensive statistics even more, many of these results are validated later—look at Speaker and Cobb in the center fielder's stats and see how they did versus each other for an example of this. When we look at players within the same era—Mantle and Mays, Cobb and Speaker, Williams and Musial, and to some extent Lajoie and Collins, and Foxx and Gehrig—they can be quite revealing.

Defensive Stats

Each player is measured against the highest score of a Hall of Famer at that position.

	Category 24 Fldg Avg	Category 25 DP/G	Category 26 A/G	Category 27 PO/G	Category 28 A as % of TC	Category 29 E as % of TC
CF	100 = .985 Snider	100 = .051 Speaker	100 = .166 Speaker	100 = 2.67 L. Waner	—	100 = .0156 Snider
RF	100 = .986 Kaline	100 = .029 Rice	100 = .121 Rice	100 = 2.12 P. Waner	—	100 = .1400 Kaline
LF	100 = .984 Musial	100 = .033 Delahanty	100 = .181 Delahanty	100 = 2.19 Goslin	—	100 = .0165 Musial
1B	100 = .992 Musial	100 = .920 Musial	100 = .770 Sisler	—	100 = 7.40 Sisler	100 = .0710 (E/G) Musial
2B	100 = .983 Schnd'st	100 = .813 Doerr	100 = 3.39 Frisch	100 = 2.66 Doerr	—	100 = .0900 (E/G) J. Robinson
SS	100 = .973 Boudreau	100 = .766 Boudreau	100 = 3.49 Jackson	100 = 2.58 Wagner	—	100 = .1410 (E/G) Aparicio
3B	100 = .971 B. Robinson	100 = .215 B. Robinson	100 = 2.28 J. Collins	100 = 1.40 J. Collins	—	100 = .0910 (E/G) B. Robinson

Defensive Stats (Outfield)

		Category 24 Fldg Avg	Category 25 DP/G	Category 26 A/G	Category 27 PO/G	Category 28 A as % of TC	Category 29 E as % of TC
Aaron	RF	.980	.014	.0720	2.00	—	.0205
	%	99.30	48.2	59.5	94.3	—	68.20
Ruth	RF	.968	.021	.0910	1.98	—	.0335
	%	98.10	72.4	75.2	93.3	—	41.70
F. Robinson	RF	.984	.012	.0630	1.86	—	.0165
	%	99.70	41.3	52.0	87.7	—	84.80
Speaker	CF	.970	.051	.1660	2.51	—	.0300
	%	98.40	100.0	100.0	94.0	—	52.00
DiMaggio	CF	.978	.017	.0880	2.62	—	.2200
	%	99.20	33.3	53.0	98.1	—	70.90
Cobb	CF	.961	.036	.1330	2.16	—	.0400
	%	97.50	70.5	80.1	80.8	—	39.00
Mays	CF	.981	.021	.0685	2.49	—	.0193
	%	99.40	41.1	41.2	93.2	—	80.80
Mantle	CF	.982	.013	.0570	2.19	—	.0179
	%	99.60	25.4	34.3	82.0	—	87.10
Musial (1,890 games)	LF	.984	.144	.0687	1.97	—	.0165
	%	100.00	42.4	37.9	89.9	—	100.00
Williams	LF	.973	.013	.0650	1.93	—	.0270
	%	98.90	39.3	35.9	88.1	—	61.10
Ott	RF	.980	.025	.1100	1.95	—	.2050
	%	99.39	86.2	90.9	91.9	—	68.29

Defensive Stats (Infield)

		Category 24 Fldg Avg	Category 25 DP/G	Category 26 A/G	Category 27 PO/G	Category 28 A as % of TC	Category 29 E as % of TC
Musial (1,016 games)	1B	.992	.920	0.60	—	7.26	.071
	%	100.00	100.00	77.90		98.1	100.00
Foxx	1B	.992	.832	0.63	—	6.98	.080
	%	100.00	90.40	81.80		94.3	88.75
Gehrig	1B	.991	.736	0.50	—	5.22	.140
	%	99.80	80.00	64.90		70.5	78.80
Lajoie	2B	.963	.515	3.07	2.650	—	.221
	%	97.90	63.30	90.50	99.60		40.72
Collins	2B	.970	.458	2.88	2.460	—	.164
	%	98.60	56.30	84.90	92.40		54.80
Hornsby	2B	.965	.571	3.30	2.050	—	.196
	%	98.10	70.20	97.30	77.00		45.91
Schmidt	3B	.955	.203	2.28	0.687	—	.141
	%	98.30	94.40	100.00	49.00		64.50
Wagner	SS	.940	.045	3.20	2.580	—	.357
	%	96.60	52.80	91.60	100.00		39.49
Morgan	2B	.981	.595	2.75	2.270	—	.096
	%	99.79	73.18	81.12	85.33		93.75
Gehringer	2B	.976	.654	3.20	2.470	—	.140
	%	99.28	80.44	94.39	91.35		64.28

The next categories are a way of measuring, according to Bill James, speed by a combination of factors.

Category 30 is Stolen Base Average as a percentage of Times on Base. Category 31 is Stolen Base Percentage. Pete Palmer offers the idea in his book, *Total Baseball*, that a stolen base percentage (not the number of stolen bases but the percentage of success) is important so you don't kill rallies and cause inning-ending outs. You would need almost a .667 percentage of success for the stolen base to be a productive play.

Category 32 is Non-HR Runs Scored as a Percentage of Times on Base. Category 33 is Grounded into Plays per game. Category 34 is Triples per game and Category 35 is Position Range—a range being defined as successful plays per game (that is put-outs, plus assists, divided by the number of games). We have to be careful here not to add first base put-outs to outfield put-outs for people who played multiple positions or we might have multiple position players such as Willie Stargell and Pete Rose being the greatest defensive players of all time. So we have calculated from the Hall of Fame fielders that the best range of a center fielder in the Hall of Fame was 2.77, right field 2.23, left field 2.23, second base 5.84, shortstop 5.97, and third base 3.43.

In Category 30, Stolen Bases as a Percent of Times on Base, Wagner, Cobb, and Collins do the best. Again, where stolen bases are presented, Joe Morgan scores high. In Category 31, Stolen Base Percentage, again Mickey Mantle and Joe Morgan score best. Percentage-wise Joe DiMaggio was a productive base stealer (with limited attempts). Charlie Gehringer scores well here, as does Willie Mays.

In Category 32, Non-HR Runs Scored as a Percentage of Times on Base, Tris Speaker does best and Gehringer and Ty Cobb score well. Now in the Times Grounded Into Double Plays per game category, obviously some of the early era statistics were not available, but of those we have, Mickey Mantle's reputation of blinding speed down to first base during his career when he wasn't hurt is validated here.

Charlie Gehringer again does well in Triples Per Game. Ty Cobb, however, has the best score with Honus Wagner doing well. Finally in Category 35, Position Range Per Game, Tris Speaker and DiMaggio again, as most baseball writers and observers would mention, covered the ground well and these numbers bear that out. Babe Ruth was considered a good outfielder by people who played with him. Here his range figures show that. Honus Wagner's reputation is validated later on in more defensive statistics, as is Charlie Gehringer's.

It would not be totally unreasonable to take these scores and average them together to see how the players rank on the basis of speed. That has been done, but that's not included in this chart. Glancing at such a summary list we find that Cobb, Wagner, Speaker, Collins, Lajoie, Gehringer, and Morgan would rank high in these speed categories followed by Mays and Mantle and then a group comprised of DiMaggio, Hornsby, Musial, and Ott. After them we would see Schmidt, Aaron, Robinson, and Gehrig and at the bottom of the list would be Foxx and Williams.

Speed

	POS	Category 30 SBA as % Times on Base	Category 31 SB%	Category 32 Non HR Runs Scored as % Times on Base	Category 33 GIDP/G	Category 34 3B/G	Category 35 Range/Position PO + A / G
Cobb	CF	23.900	.65	39.1	—	.097	CF100=2.77 2.29
	%	92.9	81.2	80.2		100.0	82.6
Speaker	CF	20.900	.57	48.7	—	.075	2.67
	%	81.6	71.2	100.0		77.7	96.3
DiMaggio	CF	1.270	.77	33.7	.102	.075	2.71
	%	4.9	96.2	69.1	46.00	77.7	97.8
Mays	CF	8.800	.80	28.0	.083	.046	2.56
	%	34.2	100.0	57.4	56.62	47.4	92.4
Mantle	CF	4.400	.48	26.4	.047	.029	2.26
	%	17.1	60.0	54.2	100.00	29.8	81.5
Ruth	RF	4.500	.77	28.2	—	.054	RF100=2.23 2.08
	%	17.5	96.2	57.9		55.6	93.2
Aaron	RF	5.600	.73	25.8	.099	.029	2.08
	%	21.7	91.2	52.9	47.40	29.8	93.2
Robinson	RF	5.800	.73	26.0	.095	.025	1.93
	%	22.5	91.2	53.4	49.40	26.4	86.5
Musial	LF	2.900	.48	27.2	.080	.058	LF100=2.23 2.04
	%	11.2	60.0	55.8	58.70	59.7	91.4
Williams	LF	0.008	.59	26.2	.085	.030	2.00
	%	3.1	73.7	53.7	55.20	30.9	89.6

Speed

		Category 30 SBA as % Times on Base	Category 31 SB%	Category 32 Non HR Runs Scored as % Times on Base	Category 33 GIDP/G	Category 34 3B/G	Category 35 Range/Position PO + A / G	
Gehrig	1B	4.30	.49	31.10	—	.074		—
	%	16.70	61.20	63.80		76.20		
Foxx	1B	3.89	.55	29.60	—	.053		—
	%	15.10	68.70	60.70		55.60		
Collins	2B	23.30	.65	36.20	—	.066	2B100=5.84	5.34
	%	90.90	81.20	74.30		68.20		91.40
Lajoie	2B	—	—	37.20	—	.065		5.73
	%			76.50		67.30		98.10
Hornsby	2B	7.20	.46	31.70	—	.074		5.36
	%	28.00	57.50	65.20		76.60		91.70
Wagner	SS	25.70	.60	35.10	—	.090	SS100=5.97	5.63
	%	100.00	75.00	72.00		92.70		94.00
Schmidt	3B	6.20	.66	18.27	.060	.028	3B100=3.43	3.0
	%	24.10	82.50	37.50	78.3	29.30		87.40
Ott	RF	—	—	29.00	—	.026		2.06
	%			59.50		26.80		91.08
Morgan	2B	18.91	.80	30.70	—	.036		5.03
	%	73.54	100.00	63.10		37.36		86.13
Gehringer	2B	6.43	.67	38.60	—	.048		5.64
	%	25.00	83.75	79.26		97.91		96.57

Now we come to the more modern statistical measurements that have helped define players beyond which the traditional statistics on the back of baseball cards have done in recent years. Looking at the definition of batting as explained in *Total Baseball* we should also know that batting wins is the measurement of runs contributed beyond those of the league's average batter or team.

So once Pete Palmer calculated how many batting runs a person contributed beyond the league average, he made a separate calculation as to the number of runs required to create an additional win beyond the average. Again we notice Ruth and Williams at the top even though this is a career statistic. Musial, Aaron, and Cobb come back up to the top. And for those looking for all around hitting and defensive players, please note through the rest of the book the closeness of Mays and Speaker in these types of measurements. With Batting Wins being a career number, Mantle and DiMaggio dropped back down, so Ruth scores the 100 points for being at the top of the list.

Category 36
Career Batting Wins

"Adjusted Batting Runs divided by the number of runs required to create an additional win beyond average. That average is defined as a team record of .500 because a league won-lost average must be .500 or as an individual record of zero because the value of the out for a given year is calculated to establish a baseline of zero."

—Total Baseball

	Score	%
Ruth.	127.5	100.00
Williams	115.9	90.90
Cobb	106.4	83.40
Musial.	99.7	78.10
Aaron	91.1	71.40
Speaker.	86.1	67.50
Mays	85.5	67.00
Gehrig.	85.4	66.90
Hornsby	84.9	66.50
Mantle.	82.9	65.00
F. Robinson.	80.7	63.20
Ott.	76.2	59.70
Foxx	75.3	59.00
Wagner	69.0	54.10
Collins.	61.9	48.50
Schmidt.	61.8	48.40
Lajoie	57.9	45.40
DiMaggio	48.6	35.70
Morgan	45.9	36.00
Gehringer	35.1	27.52

This is also a career statistic in which again we see Babe Ruth and Ted Williams at the top—power hitters first, and then Cobb and Musial; DiMaggio and Speaker move to the middle of the ranking; Morgan and Gehringer are tied. The most interesting statistic I found in this research was from a book titled *Lumber Men* by Leo Leahy. He puts forth the theory that we are frustrated in ranking players because we are always talking about different eras, comparing astro-turf players, the equipment, gloves, etc.,—the Offensive Quotient remedies the problem. Leahy talks about the fact that if you have two players who hit .300—one who hits .300 in 1968 and one who hit .300 in 1930—they are tied on paper. But in 1968 it was a pitcher's year. The National League average was .268 in 1968 and only Carl Yastrzenski hit over .300 in the American League (.301), whereas hitting .300 in 1930 is offset by the fact that the whole National League averaged over .300. (The league average was .303 in 1930). So he comes up with a formula shown on page 36 which compares the player to the League Average and creates what he has called his Offensive Quotient. Here he makes a very illuminating comparison between single season accomplishments of different years. For instance, he mentions that he can now compare Honus Wagner's hitting 4 home runs, 75 RBIs, and having a .349 batting average in 1904, which has an offensive quotient of 185. This means that Wagner played at 85 percent above the League average. Kevin Mitchell, in his MVP year of 1989, had 47 home runs, 125 RBIs, and hit .291 giving him an offensive quotient of 184, virtually the same as Wagner. So we are able to go back and look at the idea that, ranked against their peers, Wagner in 1904 and Kevin Mitchell in 1989, had similar years using the Offensive Quotient.

For instance, we spoke about the National League Average in 1930. Hack Wilson hit 56 home runs, 190 RBIs, an average of .356—a great career year for him with an Offensive Quotient of 183. Therefore, Wilson, Wagner, and Mitchell, all in their respective eras, played 83, 84, and 85 percent above the average National League batter. Now we are able to look at players across different eras and answer the question, How are we going to compare Wagner in his time with Mike Schmidt in his time?

I included the Offensive Quotient on the same page as the Total Average so you can see the similarities between the two. In other words, many of these statistics do come up with the same measurement in different ways. You will notice similarities in the rankings of Musial, Ott, and Cobb in the same position. The same six players are at the top: Ruth, Williams, Gehrig, Hornsby, Foxx, and Mantle. However in Leahy's measurement the order is slightly different. But in Leahy's measurement DiMaggio was further to the bottom than in the total average because the total average by Boswell does not measure every single at bat. Leahy took years with a minimum number of at bats and that brought DiMaggio's number down. But please note the similarity between the two lists.

Later on we will measure another one called Career Production, Category 47, which also divides the player's performance by the League's. When we reach Category 47 we'll glance at these two sets of stats and you'll see that no matter how it is measured the same "suspects" come out time after time regardless of measurement or the era. So Ruth has the 100 points on total average.

Category 37
Career Total Average

(Boswell)

$$\frac{TB + SB + BB + HBP}{AB - H + CS + GIDP}$$

	Score	%
Ruth.	1.399	100.00
Williams	1.320	94.30
Gehrig.	1.229	87.80
Foxx	1.143	81.70
Hornsby	1.105	78.90
Mantle.	1.091	77.90
Cobb	1.064	76.00
Ott.	1.036	74.05
Musial	1.028	73.40
DiMaggio	1.012	72.30
Speaker	1.011	72.20
Mays	.982	70.10
F. Robinson.	.961	68.60
Schmidt.	.954	68.10
Collins.	.940	67.10
Wagner	.940	67.10
Aaron	.940	67.10
Morgan/Gehringer	.910	65.04
Lajoie	.858	61.40

Category 37
Career Total Average

Leahy's Offensive Quotient

$$\frac{TB + BB + Outs}{League\ TB + BB + Outs} = OQ$$

Ruth
Williams
Gehrig
Hornsby
Mantle
Foxx
Cobb
Musial
Ott
Speaker
Schmidt
Mays
F. Robinson
Wagner
Aaron
DiMaggio
Lajoie
Collins
Morgan
Gehringer

The formula is illustrated and again, even being a career number and Ruth having had far fewer at bats than some of the other players, he's at the top again with Cobb, Musial, and Aaron with Williams coming in fifth. Notice in these newer statistics that we see Speaker and Mays very close, very competitive in all the rankings.

Category 38
Career Runs Created

(James)

"Bill James's formulation for run contribution from a variety of batting-base running events. Many different formulas are used, depending upon data available. In its basic expression, the formulas is:

$$\frac{(\text{Hits} + \text{Walks})(\text{Total Bases})}{\text{At Bats} + \text{Walks}}$$

The essence of this formulation is that the ability to get on base and the ability to push baserunners around fairly describes offensive ability."

—Total Baseball

	Score	%
Ruth.	2,838	100.00
Cobb	2,799	98.60
Musial	2,625	92.40
Aaron	2,550	89.80
Williams	2,538	89.40
Mays	2,372	83.50
Speaker	2,320	81.70
Gehrig	2,312	81.40
Ott	2,235	78.75
Wagner	2,218	78.10
Foxx	2,189	77.10
F. Robinson.	2,126	74.90
Hornsby	2,074	73.00
Mantle.	2,069	72.90
Collins.	2,054	72.30
Lajoie	1,895	66.70
Morgan	1,804	63.56
Gehringer	1,781	62.75
Schmidt.	1,757	61.90
DiMaggio	1,606	56.50

Career Runs Produced are defined as runs batted in plus runs scored, minus home runs. Cobb, Aaron, Ruth, and Musial top the list once again, Speaker and Mays are close together.

Category 39
Career Runs Produced

Runs batted in plus runs scored minus home runs:

	Score	%
Cobb	4,065	100.00
Aaron	3,716	91.40
Ruth.	3,669	90.20
Musial	3,425	84.20
Gehrig	3,385	83.20
Wagner	3,367	82.80
Mays	3,305	81.30
Speaker	3,294	81.00
Ott	3,208	78.91
Foxx	3,139	77.20
Williams	3,116	76.60
Collins.	3,079	75.70
F. Robinson.	3,055	75.10
Lajoie	3,020	74.20
Gehringer	3,017	74.21
Hornsby	2,862	70.40
Mantle.	2,650	65.10
DiMaggio	2,566	63.10
Schmidt.	2,553	62.80
Morgan	2,515	61.86

Devised by Bill James, Category 40, instead of just looking at gross statistics, uses modern techniques to show the won-lost record a team of nine Ruths or nine Williams would compile. Again, some pretty impressive offensive percentages when you consider how many teams win pennants with a winning percentage of .600. We have all twenty players substantially above what great teams normally achieve as a winning percentage. Ruth and Williams are at the top. Here again we find Mickey Mantle with a winning percentage over .800, Speaker and Mays are again very close together, but even in twentieth place, Charlie Gehringer has a winning percentage for his career won-lost record of .646. Most teams would love to have that!

Category 40
Career Winning Percentage

The offensive won-lost record that a team of nine Ruths
or nine Williams, etc. would compile.

	Score	%
Williams	.858	100.00
Ruth	.851	99.10
Mantle	.815	94.90
Musial	.798	93.00
Cobb	.790	92.00
Gehrig	.789	91.90
Hornsby	.784	91.30
Ott	.779	90.79
Speaker	.775	90.30
Mays	.766	90.00
Foxx	.758	88.30
F. Robinson	.758	88.30
Wagner	.752	87.60
DiMaggio	.751	87.50
Schmidt	.746	86.90
Aaron	.744	86.70
Collins	.742	86.40
Lajoie	.703	81.90
Morgan	.701	81.70
Gehringer	.646	75.29

Category 41 is the Palmer Player Rating based on his Linear Weights Measurement of a player's career. While the entire list of hundreds of players, which this is taken from, brings out some controversial comparisons, this is only our top twenty as they appear from Pete Palmer's 1991 edition of *Total Baseball.*

Category 41
Palmer Player Rating (Career)

	Score	%
Ruth.	107.9	100.00
Lajoie	92.2	85.40
Cobb	90.6	83.90
Williams	89.8	83.20
Aaron	89.6	83.00
Speaker	86.4	80.00
Mays	86.2	79.80
Wagner	80.3	74.40
Schmidt.	80.0	74.10
Hornsby	75.8	70.00
Musial.	74.9	69.40
F. Robinson.	71.2	65.90
Collins.	70.6	65.40
Mantle.	66.2	61.30
Ott.	62.4	57.83
Gehrig.	60.4	55.90
Morgan	55.7	51.62
Foxx	54.3	50.30
Gehringer	45.1	41.79
DiMaggio	44.2	40.90

In the same publication, Palmer has attempted to calculate batting runs—the runs a player created by batting beyond what the average player would have created. This category also adds fielding runs through Palmer's compilations. Fielding Runs are created from fielding plus or minus what the player would have created or lost versus the average player at his position. Then comes stolen base runs. These are also compared to what the average player would have created or lost. This system is used in Earl Weaver's *All Time Fantasy League*, an interesting book in which he played rotisserie fantasy baseball with all-time great players using this system. What we have done here is to take the batting runs, plus or minus fielding runs, plus or minus stolen bases runs, to net out a total with which to rank them. And we note that zero equals performance at the average level in that position. It has been pointed out that this system ranks batters by position. (In other words, left fielders to left fielders, and shortstops to shortstops.) When a player bats, he doesn't really bat as a shortstop, he is a batter. With all of these statistics there is agreement and disagreement on the way any one of them is set up, but generally speaking we can see some trends in the fielding that appear in two more defensive categories that we will look at later. As far as center fielders go, Tris Speaker created 245 more runs with his fielding, according to this system, than the average center fielder. Lajoie created 370 more runs than the average second baseman and Schmidt produced 265 more runs than the average third baseman. Later on in our other defensive measurements those relationships of Speaker, Lajoie, and Schmidt will be borne out. Gehrig and Hornsby measure -58 and -79, respectively. We will also see that appear again. DiMaggio, in some other stats, does better than what this statistic would say. In stolen base runs we see that Joe Morgan is 110 runs above the average player—we saw earlier how well he actually did. Willie Mays shows plus 40; noted before was the fact that Mays had the best combination of speed and power and again that comes to light in this column. Finally, we have the total number with the plus and minus netted out for ranking and again Ruth is comfortably on top.

Category 42
Total Baseball: Career Ranking
(Palmer)

Pete Palmer's system of calculating runs created by batting, fielding, and stolen bases that are above what the average player did. (0 equals average)

	Batting Runs	(+/-)	Fielding Runs	(+/-)	Stolen Base Runs	Total	%
Ruth	1,322		-6		-40	1,276	100.00
Williams	1,166		-67		-5	1,094	85.70
Cobb	1,032		+53		-10	1,075	84.20
Speaker	843		+245		-27	1,061	83.10
Musial	983		-18		-9	956	74.90
Mays	827		+86		+40	953	74.60
Lajoie	564		+370		-6	928	72.70
Schmidt	592		+265		-3	854	66.90
Aaron	878		-59		+28	847	66.30
Gehrig	918		-58		-30	830	65.00
Foxx	803		+32		-19	816	63.90
F. Robinson	773		+25		+15	813	63.70
Wagner	669		+100		-2	767	60.10
Mantle	838		-103		+23	758	59.40
Ott	767		-10		0	757	59.32
Hornsby	844		-79		-21	744	58.30
Collins	604		+48		-7	645	50.50
DiMaggio	507		+16		+4	527	41.30
Gehringer	376		+33		+1	410	32.13
Morgan	438		-205		+110	343	26.88

Category 43 uses the same formulas as Category 42, but Category 42 was career numbers and we want to also look at per game or per at bat numbers. This levels the playing field for the players with shorter careers. Even with missing time and a shorter career, Williams finished second in Category 42 with career numbers and also finished second in per game average. DiMaggio moved up at the per game level; Speaker moved up; Gehrig moved up; Cobb moved down; and Hornsby moved up. I find it interesting that with both players playing about the same number of games and having about the same number of at bats, Musial and Mays, by the time it is netted out per game, are tied with 62 points each in this study.

Category 43
Total Baseball: Career Ranking Per Game

(Palmer)

	Batting Runs Per Game	(+/-) Field-ing Runs Per Game	(+/-) Stolen Base Runs Per Game	Total	%
Ruth	.528	-.002	-.015	.511	100.00
Williams	.508	-.029	-.002	.477	93.30
Speaker	.302	+.087	-.009	.380	76.30
Gehrig	.424	-.026	-.013	.385	75.30
Lajoie	.227	+.149	-.002	.374	73.10
Schmidt	.246	+.110	-.001	.355	69.40
Cobb	.340	+.017	-.003	.354	69.20
Foxx	.346	+.013	-.008	.351	68.60
Hornsby	.373	-.034	-.009	.330	64.50
Musial	.324	-.005	-.002	.317	62.00
Mays	.276	+.028	+.013	.317	62.00
Mantle	.349	-.042	+.009	.316	61.80
DiMaggio	.292	+.009	+.002	.303	59.20
F. Robinson	.279	+.008	+.005	.288	56.30
Ott	.281	-.003	0	.278	54.40
Wagner	.239	+.035	0	.274	53.60
Aaron	.226	-.017	+.008	.257	50.20
Collins	.213	+.016	-.002	.227	44.40
Gehringer	.161	+.014	0	.175	34.44
Morgan	.165	-.077	+.041	.129	25.24

One of the most confusing aspects of all the discussions comparing baseball players is the failure to define what it is we are actually comparing. Many times we will be thinking about peak performance versus career performance thereby making it impossible to do a meaningful comparison. Bill James gives an example when he compares Sandy Koufax and Warren Spahn. With Sandy Koufax we are clearly referring to peak performance and with Warren Spahn, career performance. Another example might be Dizzy Dean and Cy Young.

So here in Category 44, we are using the same Palmer methods of Batting Runs plus or minus fielding, plus or minus stolen base runs. This time we are just taking the three best years for each player; we are incorporating this into the book because we want to show every conceivable measurement. This will represent peak performance using these formulas.

Mickey Mantle does have a higher peak performance than Willie Mays if we are making that famous comparison. Again Ruth and Williams are at the top. Please note Lajoie's numbers—he ranks third but with lower offensive numbers than the others. (But look at his middle numbers—the runs he created by his fielding.) Later on we will see evidence of his fielding prowess in the other two fielding measurements. Who else added great numbers by fielding? Speaker did very well; Schmidt did very well; Eddie Collins did very well; and Willie Mays also added numbers through his fielding.

Category 44
Total Baseball: Three Peak Years
(Palmer)

Batting Runs (+/-) Fielding Runs (+/-) Stolen Base Runs

Ruth

1921	119	+	4	-	3	=	120
1923	119	-	8	+	16	=	127
1920	113	-	0	-	4	=	109
Total							356
%							100.00

Lajoie

1901	75	+	29	+	0	=	104
1903	38	+	40	+	0	=	78
1910	68	+	17	+	0	=	85
Total							267
%							75.00

Foxx

1932	97	-	5	-	3	=	89
1933	83	+	6	-	1	=	88
1938	78	+	6	-	1	=	83
Total							260
%							73.00

Speaker

1912	73	+	21	+	0	=	94
1913	56	+	20	+	0	=	76
1914	55	+	28	-	5	=	78
Total							248
%							69.60

Hornsby

1922	90	-	7	-	2	=	81
1924	94	-	4	-	6	=	84
1925	74	+	2	+	0	=	76
Total							241
%							67.60

Williams

1941	102	-	5	-	2	=	95
1942	93	+	4	-	0	=	97
1946	94	-	1	+	0	=	93
Total							285
%							80.00

Gehrig

1927	100	-	6	-	2	=	93
1930	88	+	1	-	5	=	84
1934	86	+	1	-	0	=	87
Total							264
%							74.10

Cobb

1911	78	+	0	+	11	=	89
1915	72	+	6	-	3	=	75
1917	74	+	0	+	13	=	87
Total							251
%							70.50

Mantle

1956	83	+	2	+	2	=	87
1957	89	-	7	+	3	=	85
1961	76	-	3	+	3	=	76
Total							248
%							69.60

Musial

1948	90	+	5	-	2	=	93
1943	66	+	12	-	2	=	76
1951	70	+	6	-	2	=	74
Total							243
%							68.20

Category 44
Total Baseball: Three Peak Years
(Palmer)

Batting Runs (+/-) Fielding Runs (+/-) Stolen Base Runs

Mays

1954	62	+ 11	-	1	=	73
1955	62	+ 14	+	5	=	81
1965	65	+ 10	+	0	=	75
Total						229
%						64.30

Schmidt

1974	48	+ 26	+	0	=	74
1980	56	+ 23	+	1	=	80
1981	50	+ 23	+	1	=	74
Total						228
%						64.00

F. Robinson

1961	52	+ 8	+	5	=	65
1962	67	+ 9	+	0	=	76
1966	74	- 6	-	1	=	67
Total						208
%						58.40

DiMaggio

1937	61	+ 6	+	1	=	68
1939	56	+ 4	+	1	=	61
1941	64	+ 7	+	0	=	71
Total						200
%						56.10

Wagner

1905	52	+ 20	+	0	=	72
1908	65	- 7	+	0	=	58
1906	43	+ 24	+	0	=	67
Total						197
%						55.30

Aaron

1959	63	- 2	+	2	=	63
1963	63	- 4	+	6	=	65
1961	50	+ 12	+	2	=	64
Total						192
%						54.20

Collins

1910	33	+ 35	+	0	=	68
1913	46	+ 16	+	0	=	62
1915	52	+ 13	-	4	=	61
Total						191
%						53.60

Ott

1929	58	+ 9	+	0	=	67
1932	60	+ 2	+	0	=	62
1938	62	+ 1	+	0	=	63
Total						192
%						53.93

Gehringer

1934	48	+ 7	-	2	=	53
1936	43	+ 16	+	1	=	60
1937	44	+ 6	+	1	=	51
Total						164
%						46.06

Morgan

1972	37	- 7	+	7	=	37
1975	57	- 7	+	14	=	64
1976	61	- 23	+	13	=	51
Total						152
%						42.69

Category 45 is done for us by a friend in Los Altos, California, Bruce Winston, who, as many people do, participates in a rotisserie, or fantasy, baseball league. This formula is the one he uses when "drafting" players for the season. He volunteered this, and again, it illustrates my feelings about rotisserie baseball. If it was just on batting alone, Ruth, Williams, Gehrig, Foxx, DiMaggio, and Hornsby are the players you would want on your team for batting, but it certainly doesn't take into consideration the fielding, and it's not supposed to. But if this was the method for drafting an all-time fantasy league, here are your heavy hitters. Ruth scores 100 points.

Category 45
Rotisserie Formula (Winston)

TB + RBI + BB + SB
AB + BB

	Score	%
Ruth.	.974	100.00
Williams	.901	92.50
Gehrig	.882	90.50
Foxx	.878	90.10
DiMaggio	.828	85.00
Hornsby	.810	83.20
Mantle.	.803	82.40
Schmidt.	.791	81.20
Mays	.791	81.20
Aaron	.784	80.40
Ott.	.779	79.97
Musial.	.776	79.60
F. Robinson.	.770	79.10
Speaker	.731	75.00
Wagner	.726	74.50
Gehringer	.701	72.00
Cobb	.691	70.90
Lajoie	.689	70.80
Morgan	.686	70.48
Collins.	.681	70.00

Category 46 was done by Pete Palmer and it is simply slugging average minus batting average. We mentioned before how similar many of these measurements are. We do see the same likely suspects in roughly the same order time after time after time. Let's go back and compare Category 45 to Category 46. We see very few changes: basically the same comparisons, the same twenty names basically in the same order. So Category 45, the rotisserie formula, looks like a power measurement.

Category 46
Isolated Power

(Palmer)

Slugging Average - Batting Average

	Score	%
Ruth.	.348	100.0
Gehrig	.292	83.9
Williams	.289	83.0
Foxx	.284	81.6
Schmidt.	.260	74.7
Mantle.	.259	74.4
Mays	.256	73.5
DiMaggio	.254	72.9
Aaron	.250	71.8
F. Robinson.	.243	69.8
Ott.	.229	65.8
Musial	.228	65.5
Hornsby	.218	62.6
Gehringer	.160	45.7
Morgan	.156	44.8
Speaker	.155	44.5
Cobb	.146	41.9
Wagner	.139	39.9
Lajoie	.129	37.0
Collins.	.095	27.2

If we look at this category and, at the same time, flip back to page 36 where we have the offensive quotient also listed at the side, we see another formula of player performance divided by the League. We see Ruth, Williams, Gehrig, Foxx, Hornsby, and Mantle as the first six in this category and the same six in Category 37. In the illustrated Offensive Quotient, Musial, DiMaggio, Ott, and Cobb came in next. For those who are worried about comparing the different eras, Category 37, plus the Leahy illustration, plus Category 47 illustrates that no matter how we compare, the same individuals keep surfacing over and over.

I might add that by the time we did all 56 categories, whatever doubt there was as to who were the best players and how to rank them was gone. We just found too much evidence, over and over, for these top twenty ball players. Whichever way we cut it, the cream always comes to the top.

Category 47
Career Production

(Palmer)

Player on Base % + Player Slugging Average - 1
League on Base % + League slugging average

	Score	%
Ruth.	1.163	100.0
Williams	1.116	95.9
Gehrig.	1.080	92.8
Foxx	1.038	89.2
Hornsby	1.010	86.8
Mantle.	.979	84.1
Musial.	.977	84.0
DiMaggio	.977	84.0
Ott.	.947	81.4
Cobb	.944	81.1
Mays	.944	81.1
Aaron	.932	80.1
F. Robinson.	.929	79.8
Speaker.	.928	79.7
Schmidt.	.912	78.4
Gehringer	.884	76.0
Wagner	.855	73.5
Collins.	.852	73.2
Lajoie	—	—
Morgan	—	—

Category 48 is a measurement of peak performances by Bill James. We calculated runs that the batter created divided by how many outs he used to create these runs (i.e. runs created as a percentage of outs). Using the three best years that we could find to measure peak performance, we have Ruth and Williams leading. Mickey Mantle's peak is much higher than Willie Mays's. DiMaggio is towards the middle of the column again.

Both Category 44 and Category 48 measure the ball player in his prime (three best years).

Category 48
Runs Created as a Percentage of Outs
(Bill James)
Outs = (AB - H + CS + SH + SF + GIDP)

	Runs Created	/ Outs				Runs Created	/ Outs		
Ruth					**Williams**				
1920	211	289			1941	202	289		
1921	238	290			1946	188	354		
1923	223	338			1947	186	362		
	672 ÷	927	=	.728		576 ÷	1,005	=	.573
		%	=	100.00			%	=	79.20
Gehrig					**Mantle**				
1927	208	394			1956	188	355		
1930	195	395			1957	178	312		
1936	199	383			1961	174	360		
	602 ÷	1,172	=	.513		540 ÷	1,027	=	.526
		%	=	70.90			%	=	72.70
Foxx					**Cobb**				
1932	207	393			1911	207	354		
1933	184	386			1912	174	368		
1938	189	388			1917	165	379		
	580 ÷	1,167	=	.497		548 ÷	1,121	=	.488
		%	=	68.70			%	=	67.40
Hornsby					**Musial**				
1922	200	408			1948	191	407		
1924	186	348			1949	173	424		
1925	187	472			1951	169	394		
	573 ÷	1,228	=	.466		533 ÷	1,231	=	.432
		%	=	64.50			%	=	59.70
Speaker					**Lajoie**				
1912	175	378			1901	179	340		
1920	152	363			1904	139	374		
1923	166	387			1910	147	408		
	493 ÷	1,158	=	.425		465 ÷	1,122	=	.414
		%	=	58.70			%	=	57.30

Category 48
Runs Created as a Percentage of Outs
(Bill James)

Outs = (AB - H + CS + SH + SF + GIDP)

	Runs Created	/ Outs					Runs Created	/ Outs			
Wagner						**DiMaggio**					
1900	148	331				1937	173	424			
1905	144	356				1941	162	356			
1908	146	381				1948	140	425			
	438 ÷	1,077	=	.406			475 ÷	1,205	=	.394	
		%	=	56.10				%	=	54.40	
Ott						**Mays**					
1929	157	348				1954	157	391			
1934	150	387				1955	157	424			
1936	153	338				1958	152	413			
	460 ÷	1,173	=	.428			466 ÷	1,228	=	.379	
		%	=	58.80				%	=	52.40	
F. Robinson						**Aaron**					
1961	137	397				1959	156	434			
1962	160	437				1962	140	421			
1966	146	430				1963	149	446			
	443 ÷	1,264	=	.350			445 ÷	1,301	=	.342	
		%	=	48.40				%	=	47.30	
Collins						**Schmidt**					
1909	134	405				1974	130	426			
1912	136	393				1977	129	422			
1920	132	419				1980	137	415			
	402 ÷	1,215	=	.330			396 ÷	1,263	=	.313	
		%	=	45.60				%	=	43.30	
Morgan						**Gehringer**					
1973	128	443				1936	157	426			
1975	145	364				1934	144	408			
1976	144	344				1929	139	447			
	417 ÷	1,151	=	.362			440 ÷	1,281	=	.342	
		%	=	49.76				%	=	47.18	

This stat is what I call "Leading the League", and this answers someone who asks, How can you compare different eras? We have listed ten standard, traditional offensive categories. So for Leading the League in a year in runs scored, I gave the player 5 points; finishing second, 4 points; third, 3 points; fourth, 2 points; and fifth, 1 point. This was to measure a player's performance versus his peers. If someone is uncomfortable with comparing the dead-ball era to the 1970s, then we can look and see how a player did against his peers when they were all using basically the same gloves, playing on the same fields, under the same conditions. We see that Ty Cobb amassed 463 points. Stan Musial was second with 386, Wagner at 377, and then Ruth, Williams, and Hornsby. Again Speaker and Mays are equal with 281 points each. I would have been comfortable at stopping here with this statistic, but there are many more to do. You will notice again that the players with the shorter careers—Mantle, Schmidt, and DiMaggio—are toward the bottom in career points.

Category 50 is the same number of "Career" points earned by a player divided by their active years, usually 90 or so games as a minimum. We see Cobb still on top. Williams is moving up, Ruth is moving up, and Speaker and Mays are again very close together as DiMaggio moves up as well. Some of the more interesting (offensive) charts are included. First is Ty Cobb. In a letter he wrote March 5, 1961, responding to questions by a fan asking for the two best consecutive seasons that a player ever had, Cobb, modestly enough, offers his 1911 and 1912 seasons against "anyone, all-time." Sure enough, if we look at years 1911 and 1912, we see what he was talking about—48 total points. He led in most categories, was second only in home runs and on base percentage, and in 1912 he was first in four categories.

This point system does bear out and illustrate a player's dominance of league statistics. On the next page (Musial's chart) we notice that in 1942, Musial's first full year, he had 9 points. In 1947 he played with an appendicitis attack and played the last part of the year with his appendix frozen. Except for 1955, almost every year was a double-digit one for Musial. As most would acknowledge, 1948 was his career year and sure enough, we show a total of 44 points. For Honus Wagner we see a string of thirteen double-digit years interrupted in 1910 when he scored 9 points. For Ruth we see only 1922 and 1925 marked by personal problems, but other than those, every year that he played until 1932 was double-digits versus his peers. From these charts you can see at a glance the strengths of a player's career. Many comparisons have been made in left field between Musial and Williams. Glancing at their charts we see home runs for Williams versus triples, doubles, and total hits for Musial. Both are strong with their on base percentages and slugging averages. For Gehrig, where we noticed before those thirteen consecutive years and twelve consecutive with RBIs and runs scored, here again, from 1926 on, he had twelve uninterrupted years of double-digit points versus his peers in these categories. With Willie Mays we find (except for 1956) eleven double-digit years and then, as mentioned with the batting average, we see by this scoring system his point production falling off in 1966. Comparing Gehrig and Foxx and Musial and Williams is interesting. If we check Aaron's and Mays's tables side by side, we see similarities. Speaker's table shows one of the longest periods of time producing points versus his peers. In his last four or five years he was still competitive with his peers (doubles production and on base percentage) as is shown in this category.

Category 49
Leading the League Point System: Career

1st = 5 points, 2nd = 4 points, 3rd = 3 points,

4th = 2 points, 5th = 1 point

In the following categories

R H 2B 3B HR RBI AVG OB% SLG AVG SB

	Points	%
Cobb	463	100.00
Musial	386	83.30
Wagner	377	81.40
Ruth	344	74.20
Williams	327	70.60
Hornsby	301	65.00
Gehrig	296	63.90
Speaker	281	60.60
Mays	281	60.60
Ott	279	60.25
Aaron	274	59.10
Foxx	258	55.70
F. Robinson	231	49.80
Lajoie	222	47.90
Mantle	211	45.50
Schmidt	190	41.00
Collins	166	35.80
DiMaggio	162	34.90
Morgan	160	34.55
Gehringer	114	24.62

Category 50
Leading the League Point System:
Per Year Average

(points divided by active years)

	Per yr. points	%
Cobb	19.29	100.00
Williams	19.23	99.70
Ruth	19.11	99.00
Musial	18.38	95.20
Wagner	17.95	93.00
Gehrig	17.41	90.20
Foxx	16.12	83.50
Hornsby	15.84	82.10
Ott	15.50	80.35
Speaker	14.05	72.83
Mays	13.38	69.30
DiMaggio	12.46	64.50
Aaron	11.91	61.70
Mantle	11.72	60.70
Lajoie	11.68	60.50
F. Robinson	11.00	57.00
Schmidt	10.55	54.60
Morgan	8.00	41.47
Gehringer	7.12	36.91
Collins	6.64	34.20

Cobb

Year	Total	R	H	2B	3B	HR	RBI	Ave	OB%	SLG%	SB
1905	0	-	-	-	-	-	-	-	-	-	-
1906	0	-	-	-	-	-	-	-	-	-	-
1907	39	3	5	-	3	4	5	5	4	5	5
1908	33	-	5	5	5	-	5	5	1	5	2
1909	43	5	5	3	-	5	5	5	5	5	5
1910	38	5	4	4	-	3	4	4	5	5	4
1911	48	5	5	5	5	4	5	5	4	5	5
1912	35	5	5	-	4	4	-	5	4	5	3
1913	18	-	-	-	2	-	-	5	5	4	2
1914	0	-	-	-	-	-	-	-	-	-	-
1915	33	5	5	1	-	-	3	5	5	4	5
1916	24	5	3	-	-	-	-	4	4	3	5
1917	42	4	5	5	5	-	3	5	5	5	5
1918	32	4	4	-	5	-	1	5	5	5	3
1919	25	3	4	3	1	-	-	5	4	2	3
1920	0	-	-	-	-	-	-	-	-	-	-
1921	13	1	-	-	-	-	-	4	4	3	1
1922	18	-	4	2	3	-	2	4	3	-	-
1923	0	-	-	-	-	-	-	-	-	-	-
1924	9	4	3	-	-	-	-	-	-	-	2
1925	10	-	-	-	-	-	-	2	4	4	-
1926	0	-	-	-	-	-	-	-	-	-	-
1927	3	-	-	-	-	-	-	2	1	-	-
1928	0	-	-	-	-	-	-	-	-	-	-

463 total / 24 years = 19.29 average

Musial

Year	Total	R	H	2B	3B	HR	RBI	Ave	OB%	SLG%	SB
1942	9	-	-	-	3	-	-	4	1	2	-
1943	34	4	5	5	5	-	-	5	5	5	-
1944	29	4	5	5	1	-	-	4	5	5	-
1946	37	5	5	5	5	-	3	5	4	5	-
1947	8	2	3	-	3	-	-	-	-	-	-
1948	44	5	5	5	5	4	5	5	5	5	-
1949	38	4	5	5	4	4	3	4	5	4	-
1950	24	1	4	4	-	-	1	5	4	5	-
1951	30	5	4	-	5	1	2	5	4	4	-
1952	29	5	5	5	-	-	-	5	4	5	-
1953	23	4	4	5	-	-	-	3	5	2	-
1954	22	4	3	5	-	-	2	2	4	2	-
1955	5	-	-	-	-	-	-	3	2	-	-
1956	15	-	2	3	-	-	5	2	3	-	-
1957	21	-	-	4	-	-	3	5	5	4	-
1958	11	-	-	3	-	-	-	3	4	1	-
1959	0	-	-	-	-	-	-	-	-	-	-
1960	0	-	-	-	-	-	-	-	-	-	-
1961	0	-	-	-	-	-	-	-	-	-	-
1962	7	-	-	-	-	-	-	3	4	-	-
1963	0	-	-	-	-	-	-	-	-	-	-

386 total / 21 years = 18.38 average

Wagner

Year	Total	R	H	2B	3B	HR	RBI	Ave	OB%	SLG%	SB
1897	0	-	-	-	-	-	-	-	-	-	-
1898	0	-	-	-	-	-	-	-	-	-	-
1899	5	-	-	3	-	-	2	-	-	-	-
1900	19	-	2	3	-	-	5	2	2	-	5
1901	33	5	2	5	3	-	5	2	1	5	5
1902	38	4	3	5	4	-	2	5	5	5	5
1903	25	2	3	3	-	-	3	4	3	4	3
1904	29	5	4	5	-	-	-	5	4	4	2
1905	41	3	4	5	3	2	4	5	5	5	5
1906	29	5	4	5	-	-	-	5	4	4	2
1907	41	3	4	5	3	2	4	5	5	5	5
1908	48	4	5	5	5	4	5	5	5	5	5
1909	32	3	3	5	-	1	5	5	5	5	-
1910	9	-	5	1	-	-	1	2	-	-	-
1911	12	-	-	-	-	-	-	5	4	3	-
1912	16	-	-	3	4	-	5	1	-	3	-
1913	0	-	-	-	-	-	-	-	-	-	-
1914	0	-	-	-	-	-	-	-	-	-	-
1915	0	-	-	-	-	-	-	-	-	-	-
1916	0	-	-	-	-	-	-	-	-	-	-
1917	0	-	-	-	-	-	-	-	-	-	-

377 total / 21 years = 17.95 average

Ruth

Year	Total	R	H	2B	3B	HR	RBI	Ave	OB%	SLG%	SB
1918	12	-	-	4	-	5	3	-	-	-	-
1919	25	5	-	-	-	5	5	-	5	5	-
1920	27	5	-	-	-	5	5	2	5	5	-
1921	32	5	-	4	-	5	5	3	5	5	-
1922	8	-	-	-	-	3	-	-	-	5	-
1923	33	5	2	3	-	5	4	4	5	5	-
1924	29	5	-	-	-	5	4	5	5	5	-
1925	3	-	-	-	-	3	-	-	-	-	-
1926	29	5	-	-	-	5	5	4	5	5	-
1927	25	5	-	-	-	5	5	-	5	5	-
1928	24	5	-	-	-	5	5	-	4	5	-
1929	18	1	-	-	-	5	4	-	3	5	-
1930	24	4	-	-	-	5	2	3	5	5	-
1931	29	4	2	-	-	5	4	4	5	5	-
1932	17	-	-	-	-	4	2	2	5	4	-
1933	9	-	-	-	-	4	-	-	2	3	-
1934	0	-	-	-	-	-	-	-	-	-	-
1935	0	-	-	-	-	-	-	-	-	-	-

344 total / 18 years = 19.11 average

Williams

Year	Total	R	H	2B	3B	HR	RBI	Ave	OB%	SLG%	SB
1939	19	4	1	4	-	3	5	-	-	2	-
1940	21	5	-	2	2	-	1	3	5	3	-
1941	28	5	1	-	-	5	2	5	5	5	-
1942	33	5	3	-	-	5	5	5	5	5	-
1946	31	5	2	2	-	4	4	4	5	5	-
1947	37	5	3	4	-	5	5	5	5	5	-
1948	27	3	1	5	-	-	3	5	5	5	-
1949	38	5	4	5	-	5	5	4	5	5	-
1950	0	-	-	-	-	-	-	-	-	-	-
1951	27	2	5	-	-	4	4	2	5	5	-
1952	0	-	-	-	-	-	-	-	-	-	-
1953	0	-	-	-	-	-	-	-	-	-	-
1954	19	-	-	-	-	4	-	5	5	5	-
1955	3	-	-	-	-	3	-	-	-	-	-
1956	13	-	-	-	-	-	-	4	5	4	-
1957	19	-	-	-	-	4	-	5	5	5	-
1958	12	-	-	-	-	-	-	5	5	2	-
1959	0	-	-	-	-	-	-	-	-	-	-
1960	0	-	-	-	-	-	-	-	-	-	-

327 total / 17 years = 19.23 average

Gehrig

Year	Total	R	H	2B	3B	HR	RBI	Ave	OB%	SLG%	SB
1923	0	-	-	-	-	-	-	-	-	-	-
1924	0	-	-	-	-	-	-	-	-	-	-
1925	1	-	-	-	-	-	-	-	-	-	-
1926	12	4	-	1	5	-	-	-	-	2	-
1927	36	4	4	5	3	4	5	4	3	4	-
1928	32	4	4	4	-	4	4	3	5	4	-
1929	15	3	-	-	-	4	2	-	4	2	-
1930	30	2	4	-	3	4	5	4	4	4	-
1931	31	5	5	-	4	4	5	1	3	4	-
1932	19	2	2	-	-	2	3	4	3	3	-
1933	21	5	2	-	-	3	4	3	2	2	-
1934	32	3	4	-	-	5	5	5	5	5	-
1935	20	5	-	-	-	3	4	-	5	3	-
1936	26	5	-	-	-	5	4	2	5	5	-
1937	21	3	-	-	-	3	3	4	5	3	-
1938	0	-	-	-	-	-	-	-	-	-	-
1939	0	-	-	-	-	-	-	-	-	-	-

296 total / 17 years = 17.41 average

Mays

Year	Total	R	H	2B	3B	HR	RBI	Ave	OB%	SLG%	SB
1951	0	-	-	-	-	-	-	-	-	-	-
1952	0	-	-	-	-	-	-	-	-	-	-
1954	23	3	2	-	5	2	-	5	1	5	-
1955	32	4	-	-	5	5	4	4	1	5	4
1956	6	-	-	-	-	-	-	-	-	1	5
1957	30	3	2	-	5	2	-	4	4	5	5
1958	31	5	4	-	4	-	2	4	3	4	5
1959	15	4	-	3	-	1	-	1	1	1	5
1960	31	2	5	-	4	-	2	3	1	2	2
1961	17	5	-	1	-	4	3	-	1	2	1
1962	26	3	-	4	-	5	4	3	4	3	-
1963	15	4	-	-	-	3	1	-	3	4	-
1964	17	4	-	-	-	5	3	-	-	5	-
1965	25	4	-	-	-	5	3	3	5	5	-
1966	5	-	-	-	-	3	1	-	-	1	-
1967	0	-	-	-	-	-	-	-	-	-	-
1968	3	-	-	-	-	-	-	-	2	1	-
1969	0	-	-	-	-	-	-	-	-	-	-
1970	0	-	-	-	-	-	-	-	-	-	-
1971	5	-	-	-	-	-	-	-	5	-	-
1972	0	-	-	-	-	-	-	-	-	-	-
1973	0	-	-	-	-	-	-	-	-	-	-

281 total / 21 years = 13.38 average

Aaron

Year	Total	R	H	2B	3B	HR	RBI	Ave	OB%	SLG%	SB
1954	0	-	-	-	-	-	-	-	-	-	-
1955	9	-	4	4	-	-	-	1	-	-	-
1956	25	3	5	5	4	-	-	5	-	3	-
1957	24	5	4	-	-	5	5	2	-	3	-
1958	13	3	3	1	-	1	-	2	-	3	-
1959	26	2	-	4	-	3	3	5	4	5	-
1960	17	1	-	-	3	4	5	-	-	4	-
1961	19	3	3	5	-	-	2	1	-	3	2
1962	14	2	-	-	-	4	2	1	1	4	-
1963	32	5	3	-	-	4	5	2	4	5	4
1964	7	1	-	-	-	-	-	3	3	-	-
1965	16	-	-	5	-	-	-	4	3	4	-
1966	14	4	-	-	-	5	5	-	-	-	-
1967	21	4	-	4	-	5	3	-	-	5	-
1968	5	-	-	-	-	1	-	-	-	2	2
1969	8	-	-	-	-	4	-	-	-	4	-
1970	1	-	-	-	-	-	1	-	-	-	-
1971	16	-	-	-	-	4	3	1	3	5	-
1972	5	-	-	-	-	2	-	-	2	1	-
1973	2	-	-	-	-	2	-	-	-	-	-
1974	0	-	-	-	-	-	-	-	-	-	-
1975	0	-	-	-	-	-	-	-	-	-	-
1976	0	-	-	-	-	-	-	-	-	-	-

274 total / 23 years = 11.91 average

Mantle

Year	Total	R	H	2B	3B	HR	RBI	Ave	OB%	SLG%	SB
1951	0	-	-	-	-	-	-	-	-	-	-
1952	14	-	-	4	-	-	-	3	3	4	-
1953	3	3	-	-	-	-	-	-	-	-	-
1954	15	5	-	-	2	3	-	-	2	3	-
1955	24	4	-	-	5	5	-	-	5	5	-
1956	31	5	2	-	-	5	5	5	4	5	-
1957	24	5	2	-	-	3	-	4	4	4	2
1958	20	5	-	-	-	5	1	-	4	3	2
1959	13	4	-	-	-	2	-	-	-	3	4
1960	14	5	-	-	-	5	-	-	2	2	-
1961	20	4	-	-	-	4	1	2	4	5	-
1962	13	-	-	-	-	-	-	4	4	5	-
1963	0	-	-	-	-	-	-	-	-	-	-
1964	17	-	-	-	-	3	3	2	5	4	-
1965	0	-	-	-	-	-	-	-	-	-	-
1966	0	-	-	-	-	-	-	-	-	-	-
1967	0	-	-	-	-	-	-	-	-	-	-
1968	3	-	-	-	-	-	-	-	3	-	-

211 total / 18 years = 11.72 average

Speaker

Year	Total	R	H	2B	3B	HR	RBI	Ave	OB%	SLG%	SB
1907	0	-	-	-	-	-	-	-	-	-	-
1908	0	-	-	-	-	-	-	-	-	-	-
1909	9	-	2	-	-	-	2	-	-	1	-
1910	16	3	2	-	-	4	-	3	3	3	-
1911	5	-	-	-	-	4	-	-	1	-	-
1912	30	4	3	5	-	5	-	3	5	3	2
1913	19	-	2	4	4	-	-	3	2	3	1
1914	36	4	5	5	3	-	3	4	4	5	3
1915	8	2	2	-	-	-	-	2	2	-	-
1916	31	3	5	5	-	-	2	5	5	5	1
1917	18	-	3	4	-	-	-	3	4	4	-
1918	15	1	1	5	-	-	-	2	3	2	1
1919	4	-	-	4	-	-	-	-	4	-	-
1920	20	4	1	5	-	-	-	4	4	2	-
1921	8	-	-	5	-	-	-	1	2	-	-
1922	16	-	-	5	-	-	-	3	5	3	-
1923	28	4	4	5	-	2	5	3	3	2	-
1924	3	-	-	-	-	-	-	-	3	-	-
1925	12	-	-	-	-	-	-	4	5	3	-
1926	3	-	-	3	-	-	-	-	-	-	-
1927	0	-	-	-	-	-	-	-	-	-	-
1928	0	-	-	-	-	-	-	-	-	-	-

281 total / 20 years = 14.05 average

We return now to our second defensive category using the same system—rating players versus their peers. In Category 51, Leading the League in Fielding, we use the same approach as in the batting. This time, we compare, in one year, Hank Aaron (playing right field) against the other seven right fielders, or later the other nine or 11 right fielders who played that year. If he led those right fielders in put outs, assists, fewest errors, double plays, total chances per game, or fielding average, he would get 5 points. If he finished second, he would get 4 points. Points are not awarded after first and second place.

Some interesting facts come out. Stan Musial played over one thousand games both in the outfield and first base. In his career he accumulated 144 outfield points and 51 first base points. Therefore, to figure out his total score we take two thirds of his outfield score (he played two thirds of his games in the outfield) and one third of his first base score and are then able to get a combined score. Again, all these scores are by position. Speaker is compared against all center fielders. Musial is compared against first basemen when he played first base.

Outstanding scores come from, of course, Tris Speaker who accumulated 270 points. This is the top score (Category 51) for career total points. Divide that number by the number of active seasons he had for a yearly average of 13.5 and that is the top score. Down the list (these are not in numerical order) we see that Lajoie had 237 points at second and had a 11.85 yearly average at second base. Eddie Collins had 260 total points. Other great scores were Charlie Gehringer at second base, career and per year average. Here on the point system we see that Hornsby, Williams, Mantle, Gehrig, and Morgan accumulated fewer career points than some of the others. Again, please note the similarity between Mays and Aaron. They seem to parallel each other in a number of categories. Babe Ruth has over 100 points. Mike Schmidt has 170 career points at third base.

Let's look at some of the charts and see what those look like. Notice on Speaker's chart that he was accumulating points versus his peers at center field all the way to the end of his career, and had fourteen years where he had accumulated double-digit numbers. Note the range, the total chances per game, and how often he was among the first or second best. In double plays, of course, his style was to play very shallow center field, so shallow that he actually functioned as a pivot on second base on double plays. He had many years being the first or second in assists.

Known as a team man during his career, Stan Musial's chart shows that he did play wherever he was needed by the Cardinals. We noted earlier in the book that in only a few years Musial did not accumulate points versus his peers in fielding. In 1950, when he split the year between first base and outfield, he did not accumulate enough chances for points at either position. In 1952, the only time during his career he played center field, and his last year as a 42 year old in left field, were the only times he didn't score points. Always high in fewest errors and fielding average, he also scored in his early years in the outfield with put outs and total chances.

Looking at Willie Mays again we see him in the final seven years dropping off, similar to his batting point accumulation, but only one zero year in 1959. Mays was a sterling performer in all categories, particularly in total chances and put outs, especially considering who some of his peers were: Richie Ashburn, Vada Pinson, and Curt Flood.

Looking at Honus Wagner's chart we note that early in his career he was listed as utility, playing different positions. Articles and research from that era mention that basically whatever position he played, Honus Wagner was considered the best in that position. From the time he moved to shortstop in 1903, to his last year at shortstop in 1916, Honus Wagner never had a year where he failed to accumulate points on this system versus his peers.

With Ty Cobb's statistics we go back to his letter mentioning 1911 and 1912 as his best back-to-back years. He also mentioned that he was proud of his defensive work where he led the league in put outs, etc. Sure enough, in 1911, we see that he accumulated 19 points (on our system) and performed very well defensively.

Jimmie Foxx, as accounts have it, performed very well at first base (defensively) after starting his career as a catcher. Ted Williams's record shows only three years where he accumulated double-digits versus his peers and here we see a low score. Likewise for Lou Gehrig. We see four outstanding years for Joe Morgan, but most other years with few points. One of the most consistent performances in this system is by Eddie Collins. In fourteen years at second base he accumulated double-digit point totals versus his peers and two other years he had 9 points. Mike Schmidt validates his gold glove reputation with ten double-digit years and two 9 point years. Charlie Gehringer has an outstanding score—twelve years accumulating double-digit totals.

Category 51 and Category 52
Leading the League in Fielding Point System:
Career and Per Year Average

(Left Fielders vs. Left Fielders, Center Fielders vs. Center Fielders, etc.)

5 points for 1st place
4 points for 2nd place

PO   A   E   DP   Total Chances Per Game   Fielding Average

Name	Total Points (TP)	#51 (%)	TP / by Active Years	=	Yearly Average	#52 (%)
Speaker	270	100.00	20		13.50	100.00
Musial	144 OF	72.50	14	10.28 ⎱	9.23*	68.30
	51 1B		7	7.28 ⎰		
(10.28 x .65 + 7.28 x .35 adjusts for outfield and 1st base combined)						
Mays	174 OF	64.40	21		8.28	61.30
Aaron	171 OF	63.30	23		7.43	55.00
Wagner	160 SS	59.20	21		7.61	56.30
Cobb	159 OF	58.80	24		6.62	49.00
Ruth	118 OF	43.70	18		6.55	48.50
Collins	260 2B	96.29	20		13.00	96.29
Foxx	113 1B	41.80	16		7.06	52.30
Hornsby	98 2B	36.20	16		6.12	45.30
Williams	98 OF	36.20	17		5.76	42.60
DiMaggio	92 OF	34.00	12		7.66	56.70
Schmidt	170 3B	63.70	16		10.75	79.62
Mantle	87 OF	32.20	18		4.83	35.70
Gehrig	61 1B	22.50	17		3.58	26.50
F. Robinson	168 OF	62.20	17		9.88	73.10
Lajoie	237 2B	87.70	20		11.85	87.70
Ott	136 OF	50.37	18		7.50	55.55
Gehringer	223 2B	82.50	17		13.11	97.11
Morgan	89 2B	32.96	20		4.45	32.96

* combined average

Leading the League in Fielding
Speaker

5 points for 1st place
4 points for 2nd place

Year	Pos	Pts	PO	A	E	DP	TC/G	Fldg Avg
1907	OF	-	-	-	-	-	-	-
1908	OF	-	-	-	-	-	-	-
1909	CF	25	5	5	-	5	5	5
1910	CF	10	5	-	-	-	5	-
1911	CF	4	-	4	-	-	-	-
1912	CF	19	4	5	-	5	5	-
1913	CF	15	5	5	-	-	5	-
1914	CF	20	5	5	-	5	5	-
1915	CF	18	5	-	4	5	4	-
1916	CF	17	4	4	-	5	4	-
1917	CF	4	-	-	-	-	4	-
1918	CF	14	5	-	-	4	5	-
1919	CF	28	5	4	5	4	5	5
1920	CF	12	-	4	4	4	-	-
1921	CF	15	-	-	5	-	5	5
1922	CF	20	-	-	5	5	5	5
1923	CF	10	-	5	-	5	-	-
1924	CF	5	-	5	-	-	-	-
1925	CF	9	-	-	-	5	4	-
1926	CF	21	4	4	4	5	-	4
1927	CF	4	-	-	-	4	-	-
1928	OF	-	-	-	-	-	-	-

270 total / 20 years = 13.5 average

Leading the League in Fielding
Musial

5 points for 1st place
4 points for 2nd place

Year	Pos	Pts	PO	A	E	DP	TC/G	Fldg Avg
1942	LF	9	4	-	-	-	5	-
1943	RF	10	5	-	-	-	5	-
1944	RF	17	4	-	4	-	4	5
1946	1B	4	4	-	-	-	-	-
1947	1B	12	4	-	-	4	-	4
1948	LF	16	4	4	-	4	4	-
1949	RF	19	5	-	4	5	-	5
1950	1B/OF	0	-	-	-	-	-	-
1951	LF	13	-	4	-	4	5	-
1952	CF	0	-	-	-	-	-	-
1953	LF	9	-	-	4	-	-	5
1954	RF	18	-	4	5	4	-	5
1955	1B	8	-	-	4	-	-	4
1956	1B	8	-	-	4	-	-	4
1957	1B	10	-	-	-	5	5	-
1958	1B	5	-	5	-	-	-	-
1959	1B	4	-	-	4	-	-	-
1960	LF	9	-	-	5	-	-	4
1961	LF	14	-	4	5	-	-	5
1962	LF	10	-	-	5	-	-	5
1963	LF	0	-	-	-	-	-	-

144	OF	144 / 14 OF yrs =	10.28 x 65% = 6.68
51	1B	51 / 7 1B yrs =	7.28 x 35% = 2.54
195			9.23 combined yearly average
			(OF + 1B)

Leading the League in Fielding
Mays

5 points for 1st place
4 points for 2nd place

Year	Pos	Pts	PO	A	E	DP	TC/G	Fldg Avg
1951	CF	4	-	-	-	-	4	-
1952	CF	0	-	-	-	-	-	-
1953	CF	0	-	-	-	-	-	-
1954	CF	13	4	-	-	5	4	-
1955	CF	14	-	5	-	5	4	-
1956	CF	18	4	5	-	5	4	-
1957	CF	17	4	5	-	5	4	-
1958	CF	16	4	4	-	4	4	-
1959	CF	0	-	-	-	-	-	-
1960	CF	17	4	5	-	4	4	-
1961	CF	8	4	-	-	-	4	-
1962	CF	18	5	-	4	-	5	4
1963	CF	9	4	-	-	-	5	-
1964	CF	9	-	-	-	5	4	-
1965	CF	14	-	5	-	5	4	-
1966	CF	13	4	-	-	-	5	4
1967	CF	0	-	-	-	-	-	-
1968	CF	0	-	-	-	-	-	-
1969	CF	0	-	-	-	-	-	-
1970	CF	4	-	-	-	4	-	-
1971	CF	0	-	-	-	-	-	-
1972	OF/1B	0	-	-	-	-	-	-
1973	OF/1B	0	-	-	-	-	-	-

174 total / 21 years = 8.28 average

Leading the League in Fielding
Aaron

5 points for 1st place
4 points for 2nd place

Year	Pos	Pts	PO	A	E	DP	TC/G	Fldg Avg
1954	LF	0	-	-	-	-	-	-
1955	RF	8	4	-	-	-	4	-
1956	RF	14	-	4	-	5	5	-
1957	RF	9	5	-	-	-	4	-
1958	RF	16	4	4	4	-	-	4
1959	RF	13	4	4	-	5	-	-
1960	RF	19	5	-	-	5	5	4
1961	CF	12	-	4	-	4	4	-
1962	CF	0	-	-	-	-	-	-
1963	RF	0	-	-	-	-	-	-
1964	RF	14	-	4	-	5	5	-
1965	RF	12	4	-	-	4	4	-
1966	RF	9	-	-	-	5	4	-
1967	RF	19	5	5	-	4	5	-
1968	RF	13	5	-	-	-	4	4
1969	RF	4	-	-	4	-	-	-
1970	RF	4	-	-	-	-	4	-
1971	1B	0	-	-	-	-	-	-
1972	1B	5	-	-	-	-	5	-
1973	RF	0	-	-	-	-	-	-
1974	RF	0	-	-	-	-	-	-
1975	OF	0	-	-	-	-	-	-
1976	OF	0	-	-	-	-	-	-

171 total / 23 years = 7.43 average

Leading the League in Fielding
Wagner

5 points for 1st place
4 points for 2nd place

Year	Pos	Pts	PO	A	E	DP	TC/G	Fldg Avg
1897	CF	0	-	-	-	-	-	-
1898	1B	0	-	-	-	-	-	-
1899	OF	0	-	-	-	-	-	-
1900	RF	9	-	-	4	-	-	5
1901	UT	0	-	-	-	-	-	-
1902	UT	0	-	-	-	-	-	-
1903	SS	14	4	-	-	5	5	-
1904	SS	4	-	-	4	-	-	-
1905	SS	9	-	-	-	4	5	-
1906	SS	17	4	-	-	5	4	4
1907	SS	8	-	-	4	-	4	-
1908	SS	9	5	-	-	4	-	-
1909	SS	19	4	-	-	5	5	5
1910	SS	13	5	-	-	4	4	-
1911	SS	4	-	-	-	-	4	-
1912	SS	18	4	-	-	5	4	5
1913	SS	13	-	-	4	-	5	4
1914	SS	5	-	-	-	-	-	5
1915	SS	10	-	-	5	-	-	5
1916	SS	8	-	-	4	-	-	4
1917	1B	0	-	-	-	-	-	-

160 total / 21 years = 7.61 average

Leading the League in Fielding
Cobb

5 points for 1st place
4 points for 2nd place

Year	Pos	Pts	PO	A	E	DP	TC/G	Fldg Avg
1905	OF	0	-	-	-	-	-	-
1906	CF	4	-	-	-	-	4	-
1907	RF	14	-	4	-	5	5	-
1908	RF	18	5	5	-	4	4	-
1909	RF	15	5	5	-	5	-	-
1910	CF	8	4	-	-	-	4	-
1911	CF	19	5	4	-	5	5	-
1912	CF	0	-	-	-	-	-	-
1913	CF	4	-	-	-	4	-	-
1914	CF	0	-	-	-	-	-	-
1915	CF	4	-	-	-	4	-	-
1916	CF	0	-	-	-	-	-	-
1917	CF	14	4	5	-	5	-	-
1918	CF	8	-	-	4	-	-	4
1919	CF	8	-	-	4	-	-	4
1920	CF	4	-	-	4	-	-	-
1921	CF	9	-	5	-	-	4	-
1922	CF	8	-	-	-	4	-	4
1923	CF	0	-	-	-	-	-	-
1924	CF	18	4	-	4	5	-	5
1925	CF	0	-	-	-	-	-	-
1926	CF	0	-	-	-	-	-	-
1927	RF	4	-	-	-	-	-	4
1928	RF	0	-	-	-	-	-	-

159 total / 24 years = 6.62 average

Leading the League in Fielding
DiMaggio

5 points for 1st place
4 points for 2nd place

Year	Pos	Pts	PO	A	E	DP	TC/G	Fldg Avg
1937	CF	14	5	5	-	-	4	-
1938	CF	9	-	4	-	5	-	-
1939	CF	16	-	4	4	-	4	4
1940	CF	4	-	-	-	-	4	-
1941	CF	13	-	4	-	5	4	-
1942	CF	4	4	-	-	-	-	-
1946	CF	10	-	5	-	5	-	-
1947	CF	10	-	-	5	-	-	5
1948	CF	4	4	-	-	-	-	-
1949	OF	-	-	-	-	-	-	-
1950	CF	-	-	-	-	-	-	-
1951	CF	8	-	-	4	-	-	4

92 total / 12 years = 7.66 average

Leading the League in Fielding
Foxx

5 points for 1st place
4 points for 2nd place

Year	Pos	Pts	PO	A	E	DP	TC/G	Fldg Avg
1928	UT	-	-	-	-	-	-	-
1929	1B	9	-	-	5	-	-	4
1930	1B	5	5	-	-	-	-	-
1931	1B	5	-	-	5	-	-	-
1932	1B	9	-	-	4	-	-	5
1933	1B	9	4	5	-	-	-	-
1934	1B	17	4	4	-	4	5	-
1935	1B	10	-	-	5	-	-	5
1936	1B	-	-	-	-	-	-	-
1937	1B	14	-	5	4	-	-	5
1938	1B	8	-	4	-	4	-	-
1939	1B	12	-	-	-	4	4	4
1940	1B	5	-	-	5	-	-	-
1941	1B	10	-	5	-	-	5	-
1942	1B	-	-	-	-	-	-	-
1943	1B	-	-	-	-	-	-	-

113 total / 14 years = 8.07 average

Leading the League in Fielding
Ruth

5 points for 1st place
4 points for 2nd place

Year	Pos	Pts	PO	A	E	DP	TC/G	Fldg Avg
1918	LF	0	-	-	-	-	-	-
1919	LF	19	-	5	5	4	-	5
1920	RF	10	-	5	-	5	-	-
1921	LF	9	4	-	-	5	-	-
1922	LF	0	-	-	-	-	-	-
1923	RF	10	5	-	-	-	-	5
1924	RF	10	5	-	-	-	5	-
1925	RF	8	-	-	4	-	4	-
1926	RF	8	-	-	-	4	-	4
1927	RF	9	5	-	-	-	4	-
1928	RF	9	5	-	-	-	-	4
1929	RF	10	-	-	5	-	-	5
1930	RF	0	-	-	-	-	-	-
1931	RF	8	-	-	-	4	-	4
1932	RF	4	-	4	-	-	-	-
1933	RF	4	-	-	4	-	-	-
1934	RF	0	-	-	-	-	-	-
1935	RF	0	-	-	-	-	-	-

118 total / 18 non-pitcher years = 6.55 average

Leading the League in Fielding
Hornsby

5 points for 1st place
4 points for 2nd place

Year	Pos	Pts	PO	A	E	DP	TC/G	Fldg Avg
1916	3B	0	-	-	-	-	-	-
1917	SS	9	-	4	-	5	-	-
1918	SS	4	-	-	-	-	4	-
1919	3B	0	-	-	-	-	-	-
1920	2B	19	5	5	-	5	4	-
1921	2B	14	5	5	-	4	-	-
1922	2B	14	4	4	-	5	-	5
1923	2B	0	-	-	-	-	-	-
1924	2B	4	-	-	-	4	-	-
1925	2B	4	-	-	-	4	-	-
1926	2B	0	-	-	-	-	-	-
1927	2B	12	-	4	-	4	-	4
1928	2B	0	-	-	-	-	-	-
1929	2B	14	-	5	-	5	-	4
1930	INF	0	-	-	-	-	-	-
1931	2B	4	-	-	4	-	-	-
1932	INF	0	-	-	-	-	-	-
1933	INF	0	-	-	-	-	-	-

98 total / 16 years = 6.12 average

Leading the League in Fielding
Lajoie

5 points for 1st place
4 points for 2nd place

Year	Pos	Pts	PO	A	E	DP	TC/G	Fldg Avg
1896	1B	0	-	-	-	-	-	-
1897	1B	0	-	-	-	-	-	-
1898	2B	5	5	-	-	-	-	-
1899	2B	5	-	-	-	-	5	-
1900	2B	20	-	-	5	5	5	5
1901	2B	20	5	-	5	-	5	5
1902	2B	15	-	-	5	-	5	5
1903	2B	15	5	-	-	5	5	-
1904	2B	9	-	-	4	-	5	-
1905	2B	15	-	-	5	-	5	5
1906	2B	29	5	5	5	5	4	5
1907	2B	20	-	5	-	5	5	5
1908	2B	25	5	5	-	5	5	5
1909	2B	5	-	-	-	5	-	-
1910	2B	20	4	4	-	4	4	4
1911	2B	0	-	-	-	-	-	-
1912	2B	9	-	4	-	-	-	5
1913	2B	17	-	-	4	4	4	5
1914	2B	4	-	-	4	-	-	-
1915	2B	0	-	-	-	-	-	-
1916	2B	4	-	-	-	-	4	-

237 total / 20 years = 11.85 average

Leading the League in Fielding
Williams

5 points for 1st place
4 points for 2nd place

Year	Pos	Pts	PO	A	E	DP	TC/G	Fldg Avg
1939	RF	13	4	-	-	5	4	-
1940	LF	0	-	-	-	-	-	-
1941	LF	0	-	-	-	-	-	-
1942	LF	13	-	4	-	4	-	5
1946	LF	8	4	-	-	4	-	-
1947	LF	14	5	5	-	4	-	-
1948	LF	4	-	-	-	-	4	-
1949	LF	8	4	4	-	-	-	-
1950	LF	0	-	-	-	-	-	-
1951	LF	0	-	-	-	-	-	-
1952	LF	0	-	-	-	-	-	-
1953	LF	0	-	-	-	-	-	-
1954	LF	0	-	-	-	-	-	-
1955	LF	8	-	-	4	4	-	-
1956	LF	5	-	-	-	5	-	-
1957	LF	4	-	-	4	-	-	-
1958	LF	0	-	-	-	-	-	-
1959	LF	4	-	-	4	-	-	-
1960	LF	4	-	-	4	-	-	-

98 total / 17 years = 5.76 average

Leading the League in Fielding
Mantle

5 points for 1st place
4 points for 2nd place

Year	Pos	Pts	PO	A	E	DP	TC/G	Fldg Avg
1951	CF	0	-	-	-	-	-	-
1952	CF	10	-	5	-	5	-	-
1953	CF	0	-	-	-	-	-	-
1954	CF	9	-	5	-	4	-	-
1955	CF	14	-	4	5	-	-	5
1956	CF	9	-	4	-	5	-	-
1957	CF	4	-	-	-	4	-	-
1958	CF	5	-	-	-	5	-	-
1959	CF	18	4	-	5	4	-	5
1960	CF	8	-	-	4	-	-	4
1961	CF	0	-	-	-	-	-	-
1962	CF	0	-	-	-	-	-	-
1963	CF	0	-	-	-	-	-	-
1964	CF	0	-	-	-	-	-	-
1965	LF	0	-	-	-	-	-	-
1966	CF	10	-	-	5	-	-	5
1967	1B	0	-	-	-	-	-	-
1968	1B	0	-	-	-	-	-	-

87 total / 18 years = 4.83 average

Leading the League in Fielding
Gehrig

5 points for 1st place
4 points for 2nd place

Year	Pos	Pts	PO	A	E	DP	TC/G	Fldg Avg
1923	1B	0	-	-	-	-	-	-
1924	1B	0	-	-	-	-	-	-
1925	1B	0	-	-	-	-	-	-
1926	1B	4	4	-	-	-	-	-
1927	1B	14	5	-	-	-	5	4
1928	1B	5	5	-	-	-	-	-
1929	1B	4	-	-	-	4	-	-
1930	1B	5	-	5	-	-	-	-
1931	1B	8	4	-	-	4	-	-
1932	1B	0	-	-	-	-	-	-
1933	1B	4	-	-	-	-	-	4
1934	1B	4	-	-	-	-	-	4
1935	1B	0	-	-	-	-	-	-
1936	1B	4	-	-	-	-	-	4
1937	1B	0	-	-	-	-	-	-
1938	1B	9	4	-	-	5	-	-
1939	1B	0	-	-	-	-	-	-

61 total / 17 years = 3.58 average

Leading the League in Fielding
Morgan

5 points for 1st place
4 points for 2nd place

Year	Pos	Pts	PO	A	E	DP	TC/G	Fldg Avg
1965	2B	8	-	4	-	-	4	-
1966	2B	0	-	-	-	-	-	-
1967	2B	0	-	-	-	-	-	-
1968	2B	0	-	-	-	-	-	-
1969	2B	0	-	-	-	-	-	-
1970	2B	13	-	4	-	4	5	-
1971	2B	5	-	5	-	-	-	-
1972	2B	18	5	4	-	4	-	5
1973	2B	18	5	-	-	5	4	4
1974	2B	4	-	-	-	-	-	4
1975	2B	0	-	-	-	-	-	-
1976	2B	4	-	-	-	-	-	4
1977	2B	19	5	-	5	4	-	5
1978	2B	0	-	-	-	-	-	-
1979	2B	0	-	-	-	-	-	-
1980	2B	0	-	-	-	-	-	-
1981	2B	0	-	-	-	-	-	-
1982	2B	8	-	-	4	-	-	4
1983	2B	0	-	-	-	-	-	-
1984	2B	0	-	-	-	-	-	-

89 total / 20 years = 4.45 average

Leading the League in Fielding
Collins

5 points for 1st place
4 points for 2nd place

Year	Pos	Pts	PO	A	E	DP	TC/G	Fldg Avg
1908	2B	0	-	-	-	-	-	-
1909	2B	20	5	5	-	5	-	5
1910	2B	25	5	5	-	5	5	5
1911	2B	17	5	-	-	4	4	4
1912	2B	19	5	4	-	5	5	-
1913	2B	17	4	5	-	-	4	4
1914	2B	13	4	-	-	4	-	5
1915	2B	18	4	5	4	-	-	5
1916	2B	10	-	-	-	5	-	5
1917	2B	13	5	-	-	4	-	4
1918	2B	13	-	-	5	4	-	4
1919	2B	14	5	-	-	5	-	4
1920	2B	23	5	-	5	4	4	5
1921	2B	9	-	-	-	-	4	5
1922	2B	14	4	-	5	-	-	5
1923	2B	5	-	-	-	-	-	5
1924	2B	13	4	4	-	-	-	5
1925	2B	9	-	-	5	-	-	4
1926	2B	8	-	-	4	-	-	4
1927	2B	0	-	-	-	-	-	-

260 total / 20 years = 13.0 average

Leading the League in Fielding
Schmidt

5 points for 1st place
4 points for 2nd place

Year	Pos	Pts	PO	A	E	DP	TC/G	Fldg Avg
1973	3B	0	-	-	-	-	-	-
1974	3B	17	4	5	-	4	4	-
1975	3B	8	-	4	-	-	4	-
1976	3B	10	-	5	-	-	5	-
1977	3B	14	-	5	-	4	5	-
1978	3B	9	-	-	-	5	4	-
1979	3B	13	-	4	-	5	4	-
1980	3B	15	-	5	-	5	5	-
1981	3B	14	-	5	-	4	5	-
1982	3B	18	4	5	-	5	4	-
1983	3B	18	-	5	-	5	4	4
1984	3B	9	-	4	-	-	-	5
1985	1B	0	-	-	-	-	-	-
1986	3B	10	-	-	5	-	-	5
1987	3B	17	-	4	-	5	4	4
1988	3B	0	-	-	-	-	-	-

172 total / 16 years = 10.75 average

Leading the League in Fielding
F. Robinson

5 points for 1st place
4 points for 2nd place

Year	Pos	Pts	PO	A	E	DP	TC/G	Fldg Avg
1956	LF	8	4	4	-	-	-	-
1957	LF	29	5	5	5	5	5	4
1958	LF	22	5	4	-	4	5	4
1959	1B	9	4	-	-	5	-	-
1960	1B	10	-	-	5	-	-	5
1961	RF	17	5	4	-	4	-	4
1962	RF	15	5	-	5	-	-	5
1963	LF	9	4	5	-	-	-	-
1964	RF	12	-	-	4	4	-	4
1965	RF	8	-	-	4	-	-	4
1966	RF	4	-	-	-	-	-	4
1967	RF	13	-	-	5	4	-	4
1968	RF	0	-	-	-	-	-	-
1969	RF	0	-	-	-	-	-	-
1970	RF	8	-	4	-	4	-	-
1971	RF	0	-	-	-	-	-	-
1972	RF	4	-	-	-	4	-	-

168 total / 17 years = 9.88 average

Leading the League in Fielding
Gehringer

5 points for 1st place
4 points for 2nd place

Year	Pos	Pts	PO	A	E	DP	TC/G	Fldg Avg
1926	2B	4	-	-	-	-	-	4
1927	2B	19	4	5	-	5	5	-
1928	2B	17	4	5	-	4	4	-
1929	2B	14	5	4	-	-	-	5
1930	2B	9	4	-	-	-	-	5
1931	2B	13	-	-	5	-	4	4
1932	2B	19	5	4	-	5	5	-
1933	2B	18	4	5	-	5	-	4
1934	2B	10	-	5	-	-	-	5
1935	2B	18	4	5	-	4	-	5
1936	2B	24	4	5	-	5	5	5
1937	2B	21	4	4	-	4	4	5
1938	2B	22	5	5	-	4	4	4
1939	2B	5	-	-	-	-	-	5
1940	2B	0	-	-	-	-	-	-
1941	2B	10	-	-	5	-	-	5
1942	2B	0	-	-	-	-	-	-

223 total / 17 years = 13.11 average

Category 53 shows home runs as a percentage of strikeouts and really is an amazing statistic. Joe DiMaggio's home run total almost equals his strikeouts. How did other players do with a 300 minimum home run total? What was the trade off for home runs with strikeouts? Other home run hitting players with low strikeouts after DiMaggio are Williams, Musial, Gehrig, and Ott.

Category 53
Home Runs as a Percentage of Strikeouts

One of baseball's most amazing stats is Joe DiMaggio almost equaling his SOS (369) with HRs (361). What percentage of HRs to SOs did these players have? (300 HR minimum)

	HR	SO	%	Score
DiMaggio	361	369	97.80	100.00
Williams	521	709	73.40	75.05
Musial	475	696	68.20	69.70
Gehrig	493	789	62.40	63.80
Ott	511	896	57.03	58.28
Aaron	755	1,383	54.50	55.70
Ruth	714	1,330	53.60	54.80
Hornsby	301	679	44.30	45.20
Mays	660	1,526	43.20	44.10
Foxx	534	1,311	40.70	41.60
F. Robinson	586	1,532	38.20	39.00
Mantle	536	1,710	31.30	32.00
Schmidt	548	1,883	29.10	29.70

Category 54 is explained here as the share of the MVP voting that a person accumulated during his career in baseball. Earlier in the book we mentioned that Stan Musial won three MVPs along with other players, but each award came while he was playing at different defensive positions. We find that the four times he finished second in MVP voting he was also at different positions. In 1949 he played right field and in 1950 moved between first base and the outfield. In 1957 he played first base and in 1951 he played left field. It should be noted that this award was not available throughout Lou Gehrig's career, so without question he would also have been higher in this ranking. The sportswriters' voting was also not around during the time of Cobb, Wagner, Speaker, Ruth, Lajoie, or Hornsby.

Category 54
Bill James's Share History of
Most Valuable Player (MVP) Rating

This is Bill James's explanation of share history of MVP voting from his book, *Baseball Abstract*. If, for example, 300 votes for MVP are cast one year, and a player receives 150 votes, his "share" of the vote is 50 percent or .50. James then totals the shares of the votes a player received over his lifetime.

	Score	%
Musial	7.47	100.00
Williams	6.42	85.90
Mays	5.97	79.90
Mantle	5.72	76.50
Aaron	5.50	73.60
DiMaggio	5.46	73.00
Gehrig	5.15	68.90
Schmidt	4.88	65.30
F. Robinson	4.86	65.00
Foxx	3.80	50.80
Collins	3.58	47.90
Gehringer	3.39	45.38
Morgan	3.14	42.03
Ott	2.73	36.54
Cobb	—	—
Wagner	—	—
Speaker	—	—
Ruth	—	—
Lajoie	—	—
Hornsby	—	—

Category 55 is a point system devised by Bill James and is self-explanatory. Here we do see more of a career compilation with regard to DiMaggio and Schmidt, obviously the shorter careers, and Cobb and Aaron do much better.

Category 55
Bill James's Career Gross Value

	Score	%
Ruth	382	100.0
Cobb	351	91.8
Aaron	319	83.5
Speaker	309	80.8
Mays	301	78.7
Musial	295	77.2
Wagner	289	75.6
Williams	280	73.2
Collins	262	68.5
Ott	258	67.5
F. Robinson	252	65.9
Mantle	249	65.1
Hornsby	248	64.9
Lajoie	244	63.8
Foxx	234	61.2
Gehrig	233	60.9
Morgan	230	60.2
Gehringer	224	58.6
Schmidt	211	55.2
DiMaggio	201	52.6

This is a Point system devised by Bill James; so many points for a 20 HR season, so many points for a 30 stolen base season, so many points for a 200 hit year, etc.

We return one final time to a defensive statistic. We are again going to use Fielding Average (Fldg. Avg.), Put-outs per Game (PO/G), Assists per Game (A/G), Errors per Game (E/G),Double Plays per Game (DP/G), and Total Chances per Game (TC/G). But this time we measure a player's performance in a year versus anyone in that position that year. This is similar to the Offensive Quotient discussed earlier. In 1910, Ty Cobb, in 137 games, had a fielding average in centerfield of .958. All the other centerfielders averaged .959. Cobb's percentage .958, divided by the league's percentage .959, equals .998. Cobb's fielding average was therefore 99.8 percent compared to the other center fielders. His put-outs per game were 2.27 versus 1.92 for the other center fielders. (2.27 divided by 1.92 equals 1.182) (1.00 equals the position average). In other words, Cobb was 18.2 percent better than the others. Each score is weighted by the games played (154 game season total is obviously worth more than a 41 game total) and then all six career totals are averaged for a final score. As shown by the enclosed work sheet, Cobb, for his career, fielded at an average of .996 of his position's fielding average. At PO/G, his score was 1.025 or + 2.5 percent. At Assists per Game he had 1.010, or + 1.0 percent. With Errors per Game (here we reversed the division because the fewest errors are best) he had 1.028, or + 2.8 percent; in DP/G he had 1.319, or + 31.9 percent; in TC/G he was 1.012, or + 1.2 percent. For his twenty-four years calculating each stat in each year, his average score was 1.065, or + 6.5 percent. Ty Cobb fielded 6.5 percent better for his career than all the players at his position.

Speaker and Lajoie live up to their reputations as great fielders. Frank Robinson seems to be a generally overlooked player. I have broken out the scores for Stan Musial—outfield and first base only—and the score that was counted in the report, the combined total. As noted by his contemporaries, Ruth was a good outfielder (+2.3 percent). Mantle's score, while surprising to some, we will remember is a career number. His non-injury years—'55, '56, '61 etc., are much better.

This category finally broke the log jam at second base, the final finish of Lajoie, Hornsby, Collins being decided in the last category. Only four players, Speaker, Lajoie, Wagner, and Gehringer, scored 1.0 or above in every fielding category for their career. Willie Mays scored .999 in career fielding average versus his peers or he also would have been 1.0 or better in every category. As the Cobb sample shows, this category was the most work, but I believe it most accurately indicates career defensive ability in relation to a player's peers.

Cobb OF

Games	Year	Fldg Avg	PO/G	A/G	E/G	DP/G	TC/G
41	1905	$\frac{.958}{.964}$ .993	$\frac{2.31}{1.96}$ 1.178	$\frac{.146}{.126}$ 1.158	$\frac{.097}{.077}$ .793	$\frac{.024}{.039}$ .615	$\frac{2.31}{2.17}$ 1.064
96	1906	$\frac{.961}{.961}$ 1.000	$\frac{2.16}{2.01}$ 1.074	$\frac{.145}{.125}$ 1.160	$\frac{.093}{.084}$ .903	$\frac{.041}{.033}$ 1.242	$\frac{2.40}{2.22}$ 1.081
150	1907	$\frac{.961}{.963}$ .997	$\frac{1.63}{1.47}$ 1.108	$\frac{.205}{.137}$ 1.496	$\frac{.073}{.062}$ .843	$\frac{.082}{.044}$ 1.863	$\frac{1.90}{1.63}$ 1.165
150	1908	$\frac{.944}{.950}$ .992	$\frac{1.45}{1.36}$ 1.066	$\frac{.157}{.132}$ 1.189	$\frac{.093}{.075}$ .806	$\frac{.034}{.038}$ .894	$\frac{1.70}{1.98}$ .858
156	1909	$\frac{.946}{.959}$ .986	$\frac{1.46}{1.39}$ 1.050	$\frac{.157}{.140}$ 1.121	$\frac{.089}{.096}$ 1.078	$\frac{.046}{.029}$ 1.586	$\frac{1.70}{1.60}$ 1.062
137	1910	$\frac{.958}{.959}$ .998	$\frac{2.27}{1.92}$ 1.182	$\frac{.131}{.164}$ .798	$\frac{.102}{.087}$ .852	$\frac{.029}{.044}$ .678	$\frac{2.5}{2.17}$ 1.152
146	1911	$\frac{.957}{.960}$ .996	$\frac{2.61}{2.23}$ 1.170	$\frac{.166}{.166}$ 1.000	$\frac{.123}{.092}$ .747	$\frac{.069}{.040}$ 1.736	$\frac{2.90}{2.50}$ 1.160
140	1912	$\frac{.940}{.951}$ .988	$\frac{2.29}{2.14}$ 1.070	$\frac{.148}{.154}$ .967	$\frac{.157}{.120}$ .764	$\frac{.035}{.041}$ .864	$\frac{2.60}{2.41}$ 1.078
119	1913	$\frac{.947}{.949}$ .997	$\frac{2.18}{2.14}$ 1.018	$\frac{.183}{.158}$ 1.158	$\frac{.134}{.125}$ .932	$\frac{.066}{.038}$ 1.754	$\frac{2.50}{2.42}$ 1.033
96	1914	$\frac{.949}{.957}$ .991	$\frac{1.82}{2.21}$ .823	$\frac{.082}{.132}$ .624	$\frac{.104}{.102}$ .980	$\frac{0}{.029}$ 0	$\frac{2.00}{2.43}$ .823
156	1915	$\frac{.951}{.962}$ .988	$\frac{2.14}{2.32}$ .922	$\frac{.143}{.142}$ 1.012	$\frac{.115}{.096}$ .834	$\frac{.045}{.025}$ 1.830	$\frac{2.40}{2.56}$ .937
143	1916	$\frac{.953}{.969}$ .983	$\frac{2.25}{2.31}$ .977	$\frac{.125}{.142}$ .880	$\frac{.118}{.076}$ .644	$\frac{.062}{.044}$ 1.409	$\frac{2.50}{2.53}$ .988
152	1917	$\frac{.973}{.972}$ 1.001	$\frac{2.45}{2.39}$ 1.025	$\frac{.177}{.139}$ 1.277	$\frac{.072}{.070}$ .972	$\frac{.059}{.033}$ 1.794	$\frac{2.70}{2.57}$ 1.050

Cobb OF

Games	Year	Fldg Avg	PO/G	A/G	E/G	DP/G	TC/G
95	1918	$\frac{.975}{.969}$ 1.006	$\frac{2.41}{2.36}$ 1.021	$\frac{.129}{.166}$ .777	$\frac{.063}{.081}$ 1.285	$\frac{.010}{.028}$ .384	$\frac{2.60}{2.60}$ 1.000
123	1919	$\frac{.973}{.957}$ 1.016	$\frac{2.19}{2.40}$ .913	$\frac{.153}{.143}$ 1.071	$\frac{.065}{.109}$ 1.676	$\frac{.024}{.039}$ .620	$\frac{2.40}{2.63}$ .912
112	1920	$\frac{.966}{.966}$ 1.000	$\frac{2.15}{2.38}$ .906	$\frac{.070}{.122}$ .575	$\frac{.080}{.085}$ 1.062	$\frac{.017}{.033}$ .531	$\frac{2.30}{2.58}$ .891
121	1921	$\frac{.970}{.963}$ 1.007	$\frac{2.50}{2.47}$ 1.012	$\frac{.225}{.133}$ 1.691	$\frac{.082}{.097}$ 1.182	$\frac{.016}{.025}$ .666	$\frac{2.80}{2.70}$ 1.037
134	1922	$\frac{.980}{.969}$ 1.011	$\frac{2.44}{2.40}$ 1.018	$\frac{.103}{.111}$ .927	$\frac{.052}{.080}$ 1.538	$\frac{.022}{.023}$ .966	$\frac{2.60}{2.63}$ .988
141	1923	$\frac{.969}{.970}$ .998	$\frac{2.62}{2.50}$ 1.049	$\frac{.101}{.108}$ .939	$\frac{.085}{.078}$ .917	$\frac{.086}{.024}$ 3.623	$\frac{2.80}{2.68}$ 1.044
155	1924	$\frac{.986}{.978}$ 1.008	$\frac{2.69}{2.62}$ 1.026	$\frac{.077}{.095}$ .814	$\frac{.038}{.059}$ 1.552	$\frac{.051}{.015}$ 3.440	$\frac{2.80}{2.77}$ 1.010
105	1925	$\frac{.948}{.970}$ .977	$\frac{2.59}{2.75}$ .942	$\frac{.087}{.091}$ .960	$\frac{.142}{.085}$ .598	$\frac{.009}{.035}$ .277	$\frac{2.80}{2.93}$ .955
55	1926	$\frac{.950}{.962}$ .987	$\frac{2.01}{2.06}$ .975	$\frac{.074}{.083}$ .891	$\frac{.109}{.072}$ .660	$\frac{.037}{.020}$ 1.85	$\frac{2.20}{2.58}$ .852
127	1927	$\frac{.969}{.961}$ 1.008	$\frac{1.97}{1.88}$ 1.047	$\frac{.073}{.107}$ .682	$\frac{.062}{.070}$ 1.129	$\frac{.019}{.032}$ .593	$\frac{2.10}{2.07}$ 1.014
85	1928	$\frac{.964}{.972}$ .991	$\frac{1.85}{1.84}$ 1.005	$\frac{.084}{.102}$ .823	$\frac{.038}{.075}$ 1.973	—— 0	$\frac{2.02}{2.00}$ 1.000
2935		2925.907	3010.807	2966.412	3018.709	3873.527	2973.121
1.065		**.996**	**1.025**	**1.010**	**1.028**	**1.319**	**1.012**

Category 56
Career Defensive Ability Versus Peers

(1.0 equals the position average)

	Score		%
*Speaker	1.2170	(+21.70%)	100.00
*Lajoie	1.1720	(+17.20%)	96.30
Ott	1.1270	(+12.70%)	92.61
Mays	1.1110	(+11.10%)	91.29
Schmidt	1.1030	(+10.30%)	90.63
F. Robinson	1.0930	(+9.30%)	89.81
DiMaggio	1.0890	(+8.90%)	89.48
Musial (outfield only)	1.0860	(+8.60%)	—
Collins	1.0840	(+8.40%)	89.07
Musial (OF and 1B)	1.0740	(+7.40%)	88.24
*Wagner	1.0650	(+6.50%)	87.51
Cobb	1.0650	(+6.50%)	87.51
Morgan	1.0650	(+6.50%)	87.51
*Gehringer	1.0530	(+5.30%)	86.53
Musial (1B only)	1.0528	(+5.28%)	—
Aaron	1.0525	(+5.25%)	86.48
Williams	1.0470	(+4.70%)	86.03
Foxx	1.0370	(+3.70%)	85.20
Ruth	1.0230	(+2.30%)	84.05
Mantle	.9920	(-.80%)	81.51
Hornsby	.9710	(-2.90%)	79.78
Gehrig	.9570	(-4.30%)	78.63

* Finished above 1.0 in every category: Fldg. Avg., PO/G,
A/G, Fewest E/G, DP/G, and TC/G.

Twenty Greatest Careers/Final Standings

	Name	Points	/	Categories	=	Score
1.	Ruth	4,225.86		53		79.73
2.	Cobb	4,056.30		52		78.00
3.	Speaker	3,995.03		52		76.82
4.	Musial	4,387.14		60		73.11
5.	Wagner	3,672.40		52		70.62
6.	Williams	3,880.83		55		70.56
7.	Gehrig	3,698.82		53		69.78
8.	Mays	3,754.39		55		68.26
9.	Foxx	3,566.42		53		67.29
10.	Aaron	3,692.25		55		67.13
11.	Lajoie	3,167.32		48		65.98
12.	Hornsby	3,475.85		53		65.58
13.	Collins	3,470.93		53		65.48
14.	Ott	3,398.80		52		65.36
15.	F. Robinson	3,469.00		55		63.07
16.	Gehringer	3,305.65		53		62.37
17.	Schmidt	3,396.08		55		61.74
18.	Mantle	3,373.91		55		61.34
19.	DiMaggio	3,357.47		55		61.04
20.	Morgan	3,073.16		52		59.09

Separate ranking of catchers in the same categories:

	Name	Points	/	Categories	=	Score
1.	Berra	2,700.96		51		52.94
2.	Cochrane	2,545.64		50		50.91
3.	Dickey	2,526.60		50		50.53
4.	Bench	2,423.90		51		47.52

Appendix

Number of Times a Player Led the League

(in the following offensive categories:
R H 2B 3B HR RBI BA OB% SLG% SB)

(and in the following fielding categories:
PG A E DP TC/G and Fldg. Avg.)

	Fielding	+	Batting	=	Total
Cobb	15		55		70
Lajoie	37		30		67
Ruth	14		49		63
Musial	19		42		61
Wagner	16		44		60
Speaker	38		18		56
Hornsby	10		42		52
Williams	5		45		50
Schmidt	18		21		39
Collins	27		9		36
Mays	15		21		36
Gehringer	27		8		35
Aaron	15		19		34
Foxx	13		20		33
F. Robinson	16		15		31
Mantle	11		18		29
Gehrig	5		21		26
Ott	8		15		23
Morgan	10		7		17
DiMaggio	8		9		17

Number of Times a Player Appeared in the Top 5 of Any Category in This Report

	Total Times in Top 5	=	By Offensive Category	+	By Defensive and Range Category	+	By Speed and Range
Ruth	32		31		1		0
Musial	26		18		7		1
Williams	26		26		0		0
Cobb	24		21		0		3
Speaker	21		12		5		4
Gehrig	20		18		1		1
Wagner	15		10		1		4
Aaron	14		12		1		1
Foxx	12		11		1		0
Lajoie	11		5		4		2
Mantle	11		7		2		2
Mays	10		6		1		3
Collins	9		5		2		2
DiMaggio	9		5		1		3
Ott	8		3		4		1
Gehringer	8		2		3		3
Hornsby	7		5		1		1
Morgan	7		4		2		1
Schmidt	6		3		2		1
F. Robinson	2		1		1		0

An All-Time All-Star Team Chosen From This Report

Ruth—RF*
Cobb—CF*
Speaker—CF
Musial—LF*
Wagner—SS*
Williams—LF
Gehrig—1B*
Mays—CF
Foxx—1B
Aaron—RF
Lajoie—2B*
Hornsby—2B
Collins—2B
Ott—RF
F. Robinson—RF
Gehringer—2B
Schmidt—3B*
Mantle—CF
DiMaggio—CF
Morgan—2B

Catchers
Berra*
Cochrane
Dickey
Bench

*Denotes highest score at position

If we scan the final standings, noting the primary positions of the players and take the highest score by position, we can easily make a formidable batting order:

Cobb—CF

Wagner—SS

Musial—LF

Ruth—RF

Gehrig—1B

Schmidt—3B

Lajoie—2B

Berra—C

For pitching, if we refer to other authors such as Ralph Horton, Bill James, and Pete Palmer on pitching rankings, a consensus would be to pick:

Walter Johnson—RHP

Lefty Grove—LHP

While we are at it, let's use Ted Williams as our pinch hitter, Tris Speaker as late inning defensive help, and John McGraw as our manager.